Praise for *Le...*
and Shari Owen Brown

"Shari Owen Brown is a rare breed of leader who can be both extremely relatable and aspirational. I've seen Shari inspire and lead with an unbreakable spirit focused on helping others accomplish their goals, not her own. I've always said that the secret to success for a leader is to care more about the success of others than their own, and no one exemplifies this more than Shari. I'm very blessed to have had Shari as a top leader in our company for the past many years and look forward to many more."

DEREK MAXFIELD, Younique founder and CEO

"I had just started my business and was clueless as to where to start. I came across a video of a woman demonstrating products in her bathroom. She was magnetic and real, and I immediately knew I could do this. Shari Owen Brown gave me the courage to start exactly as I am through that one authentic video, and my life literally changed forever. She has continued to help me grow professionally and personally through her trainings and teachings. I would not be where I am today without her mentorship."

KARA LEWIS NEWTON, award-winning top-level leader

"*Let's Grow, Girl!* is a breath of fresh air! Shari Owen Brown has a way of making what we do in this industry simplified and human. Women need more of this-— encouragement to build a sustaining business in a way that is duplicatable and attainable for anyone! It truly is a playbook. I will be recommending it to all of my team members!"

SHAWN MICHELLE NELSON, award-winning top-level leader

"Shari Owen Brown is the leader of leaders! Her combination of authenticity, humor, and a no-nonsense approach to your business and your life makes her a woman to follow, model, and learn from. Her stories and humor are her signature teaching style, and reading this book is like having Shari at your kitchen table! Whether you're trying to learn how to build a large team or balance it all, Shari will pull from her successes and failures, and guide you through growth with ease and laughter."

TORI POULTER, Younique EVP
Presenter Experience and certified coach

"Shari Owen Brown just has a way of making you feel like she's talking to her best friend! Her witty sense of humor mixed with her relatable stories make for a fun, easy read packed full of useful and practical tips to apply to your business (and life)! She captivated me with her words, drew me in, and kept me wanting to read, so I could hear more! Anyone in this business *needs* to read this book!"

KARLEE PRINS, award-winning top-level leader

Your Network
Marketing Playbook Where
You Get Paid to Be You

SHARI OWEN BROWN

Let's Grow *Girl!*

PAGE TWO

Cataloguing in publication information is
available from Library and Archives Canada.
ISBN 978-1-77458-072-1 (paperback)
ISBN 978-1-77458-215-2 (ebook)
ISBN 978-1-77458-229-9 (audiobook)

Page Two
pagetwo.com

Edited by Kendra Ward
Copyedited by Christine Lyseng Savage
Proofread by Jennifer D. Foster
Cover and interior design by Fiona Lee
Interior illustrations by Fiona Lee

sharibrown.com

To D, K, and A,
you're the wind beneath my lashes. xo

Contents

Making It Up as You Grow 1

PART ONE **THE MINDSET: Your Growth Starts Here**

1   **What Makes You Weird Is Your Greatest Gift** 15

2   **From Insecurities to Influence and Impact** 33

3   **Fear of Regret vs. Fear of Failure** 45

4   **Everything Is Always Working Out for You** 57

5   **You Win or You Learn** 73

PART TWO **MAKING MONEY: The Modern-Day Handbook for Selling Success**

6   **Cannonball!** 89

7   **Houston, You Have a Networking Problem** 103

8   **The Art of Non-selling** 125

9   **Duplication Nation! How to Build a Business** 151

10   **Big Whoop!** 167

Grow for It! 183

Acknowledgments 191

Making It Up as You Grow

THE HEAVING sobs had finally stopped, and I laid there in silence, feeling numb. I was on the floor of my tiny condo, having just cried my eyes out for over an hour. In five days my mortgage payment was due, and I had $24 to my name, with no income in sight. That morning all 15 of my massage clients that I had booked for the entire week called and cancelled. Every. Single. One. All within two hours. *What* was happening?! Was this a joke? How is this even possible? It was Monday, and I owed an $850 mortgage payment by Friday. I was barely going to make the payment as it was, even *with* the 15 clients I had booked, but now... I had nothing.

I didn't know what to do, and I don't know where the idea even came from, but for the first time in my life, I sat in stillness and meditated. To be honest, I really didn't even know that that was what I was doing at the time. I just knew I had to calm the hell down... and I had no energy to get up off the floor.

I thought to myself, "Okay, in *this* moment I have a roof over my head. In *this* moment I have food in my fridge. In *this* moment my bills are paid, and I have good credit." (Good credit was a big deal to me! Still is.) I just kept repeating this over and

1

over, and finding things to be grateful for to calm myself from the incredible fear of what would happen when Friday came and I couldn't pay my mortgage. I couldn't believe that this was how it was all going to end! Slowly, the meditation started to work, and I felt a bit better.

Just two months earlier, I had taken a huge risk by buying a condo. I was a self-employed massage therapist who was determined to live alone without roommates, a plan I was *seriously* rethinking at that moment. A chance run-in with an old friend, who was a mortgage lender, led me to buying a place, albeit tiny, with almost no money down. My income wasn't much, but it had been steady, up until that point. "I can buy a condo on my own. It will be fine. I have faith." Well, that faith was now being put to the test. Being able to buy the world's smallest condo in Southern California was a true miracle, and I couldn't believe that something so incredible could happen, only to leave me practically destitute two months later.

As I look back on that day, I realize that by repeating the mantra of "In *this* moment I have a roof over my head" and so on, I was bringing myself into the present moment. Nothing bad had happened . . . *yet*. I knew it was coming, but in that actual *moment* I was okay. I needed to get rid of the horrible feeling of doom that I had sitting on my chest, and for some reason, I decided to visualize Oprah Winfrey knocking on my door and writing a check to pay off my bills. *All* my bills! #thanksO You see, at that moment in my life, it was more likely that Oprah herself would knock on my door and give me money than it was for me to find a job that paid me enough to do it myself. By the way, I was earning a whopping $14,000 per year as a massage therapist, so you can see why it was so hard for me to imagine. #livinthedream

Sitting on the floor and visualizing all of my bills being paid, I physically felt a weight lifting off me. I felt lighter. I felt calmer. I felt free. I decided that Friday was going to suck *hard*, but since there was nothing I could do to stop it from coming, I might as well enjoy the next four days before it all hit the fan. But guess what happened? Miraculously, by Friday I had *exactly* $850 in my bank account, and I made my payment! On Thursday my phone randomly started ringing off the hook with customers wanting gift certificates. Just like the two-hour mad rush of phone calls cancelling appointments on Monday, Thursday was a mad rush of gift certificate *orders*. I had just witnessed *two* miracles in less than a week!

The timing of the cancellations and the orders was not lost on me. I knew that the odds of either one of those things happening within such a short time span was no mistake. It was meant to get my attention, and boy did it ever. I knew there was something in that situation that I was supposed to notice and learn from, and my best guess was that God was teaching me to trust. I know now that He was teaching me the beginnings of one of my biggest life lessons and something I now say to myself daily: "Everything is always working out for me." You really don't have a choice but to trust when the rug is pulled out from under you and it's all in God's hands. But I guess I could have continued to wail and wallow. Instead, I chalked it up to a lesson learned, thanked the good Lord that it was over, and prayed it would never happen again.

Well, it did. Over... and over... again. It got to the point where the stream of calls to cancel appointments wouldn't even phase me. I mean, it was definitely an adrenaline rush each time, but this happened so often that it was getting ridiculous and predictable. It felt like I was being punked by the Universe. *Come on, already!* I get it, you're funny... you're *hilarious*. You're teaching me that I'm being watched over and it's going to be okay... so can we stop now? But no, it went on for years. Ebb and flow, taken and given; it's just how I learned to roll. I

You're made of tough stuff, whether you think so right now or not. **Your best is yet to come.**

always had just enough but wondered if there would ever be a time when I would have a little extra.

Little did I know that 14 years later, I would become a millionaire.

I credit that breakdown, that lesson, and that meditation as the beginning of my path to a multimillion-dollar manifestation. I have paid close attention to all the lessons I've learned over the years, and I've spent countless hours reflecting back on what led to this incredible life that I'm living today. I am so excited and grateful to be able to share these lessons with you!

I'm sure you've got your own stories of being at the end of your rope, convinced that everything was going to fall apart— and yet here you are, surviving and carrying on with life! All those lessons and scars have made you into the person you are today. So take a moment to appreciate your strength and perseverance. You're made of tough stuff, whether you think so right now or not. Your best is yet to come!

I WROTE this book because I wanted to share some of these revelations and tools with you. I've always felt like one reason I became my company's first millionaire was because God knew I had a big mouth. He knew that when I discovered something that could help others, I was going to shout it from the rooftops. My big mouth is what built my online business. When I discovered a strategy that worked, I shared it with everyone. I am a teacher at the core of my being, and I love nothing more than sharing my favorite find or technique with thousands of my closest friends. I live with zero fear that if I share what I know, someone will take it or use it and I will have less. I don't believe that is how the Universe works. To get more, you give more. It's through sharing that I have found my greatest achievements and blessings. This book is just another way for me to shout from the rooftops, so I appreciate you being here to "listen"!

One thing you'll discover in the pages of this book is that there's no magic pill or process to developing a successful network marketing business. #sorryCharlie It's like a gym membership; you've still gotta do the work! But I think you're going to be pleasantly surprised to see that it's equal parts mindset and skill, and it's much simpler than you might think. That's why I've split this book up into two parts. The first part is all about the mindset you're going to need to build your business. I can't tell you how many women I've coached who have had tremendous skills, but they just couldn't make things happen because their head got in the way! Self-sabotage took them out of the game before they even had a chance. Well, you're not going to go down like that—not on my watch! #Igotyou I dug way back into the archives of my life and found the key moments that taught me lessons that I believe were the foundation of my success. It is my hope and expectation that they will trigger something within you to help you move past fear and into action. I've also shared stories of some of the women I've coached over the years and how they overcame some very common challenges.

Once we make sure your head's in the right place, we move on to Part 2, some fundamentals on how to make money and grow your skills! I mean, that is why you're here, right? Psst. Did you know that it's okay to want to make money? Because without it we are sobbing uncontrollably on the floor in the fetal position, remember?! Let's not go there again!

Practice makes progress, so just like learning to swim, you can't read a book about it and not jump in the pool! Take what speaks to you here and put it into practice. You're going to learn ten times more when you read and then *do* than you would by just reading. You're building your money-making muscles— and the techniques are simple, but they aren't always easy. We will be tapping into the mindset piece a lot to remind you that you can do *anything* you set your mind to. Even if nobody has ever told you so, I'm telling you now. You've got this!

No matter what your situation is right now, you have the power to create amazing things. Whether you're a stay-at-home mom rubbing nickels together to make ends meet (#beenthere), are working full-time and need extra money to make ends meet (#beentheretoo), or just want some fun money that's all your own, *decide right now* that you can have it!

I have said for years that I don't have anything in me that someone else doesn't have or couldn't have. I'd like to tell you that I had every intention of building a $600 million online network marketing business, but honestly, it's as much of a shock to me as it is to anyone else. In fact, in that first year of building my business, I often heard women say that they joined my team because they thought, "If this chick can do it, I can do it!" (Sidebar: Turns out that being relatable is a huge factor in duplication within your business, so don't worry about being perfect. Perfection is not your friend!)

There is a joke within the company that my initial goal was to earn enough money for a mani/pedi once a month. It's true! When I earned that money in the first 48 hours of joining, I was *overjoyed*, and any money earned after that was a *bonus*. So yes, that was the secret sauce to my success—complete and absolute mediocrity! It's sort of my shtick now. *Aim low, people!!* #watchoutTonyRobbins #mediocreworldtour

But seriously, when you hit those small goals, the rest is gravy. It's pure joy! The gratitude for the gravy will attract more gravy. Cue the mashed-potato parade!

Before beginning my network marketing career in July 2013, I had been a stay-at-home mom for eight years. It was very important for me to be home with my children, who were then seven and four years old. I'd like to tell you that being a stay-at-home mom was fulfilling and rewarding and checked all the boxes for me. It wasn't. I was coming apart at the seams. I was desperate for any ounce of alone time or something to stimulate my brain. I was stressed over money because at that time we only had $100 left at the end of the month, after all the bills were paid. That money had to cover any dining out, including pizza, McDonald's, ice cream, movies, any extra stuff. It didn't go far!

I remember that back then, if both kids needed shoes in the same month, which *always* seemed to happen, I would have to buy one kid's shoes at the end of one month and make the other kid wait until the first of the next month. (Okay, but seriously, *how* is it that they always needed shoes at the same time?!) And when it came time for Halloween costumes, I'd have to start searching in August so I could spread out the expense. Same with Christmas! Christmas shopping started in the summer. If I found a good deal on something at any time of the year, if I had the money to buy it, I'd grab it and put it away for the next holiday. I had all sorts of strategies for saving money and stretching a dollar.

But the time came when my youngest was four years old, and just when I thought I couldn't be any more stressed out, my husband said, "You know, when he starts kindergarten, you need to get a job to help pay the bills." I could feel my blood pressure rising... or was that my lunch? What on *earth* could I do during school hours that would pay me more than $15 per hour? I had to be there for drop-off and pickup... and what if they were sick? What about volunteering in the classroom? (I had to throw that one in there because when they were little, I tried so hard to be the good mom and volunteer—but as it turns out, that's not my thing. Like *not* my thing *at all*. I'd rather have a root canal. Lol.) #butseriously So when my friend Tami told me about her network marketing business for the hundredth time, I was finally in. I didn't really know what was possible, but I thought *any* extra money could help us out. The rest, as they say, is history.

Approach your life with **a spirit of *go*!**

Before I started my business, if you had asked me why so many people struggle financially, I would have responded *immediately* with, "Because there just aren't enough opportunities out there." I was the girl who watched infomercials about stuffing envelopes for ten cents each. When I factored in the cost of the bandages that I would need from all those paper cuts, I gave up on that idea. I was always on the lookout for any opportunity to make some money. I even made jewelry at one point, sold purses, and thought about making candles—you name it, I considered it!

That all changed when I discovered the magical combination of network marketing and social media. I was *so excited*; I couldn't wait to tell everyone I knew about it! I didn't care how I sounded or how it came across; I had found a *gold mine*, people! It was full steam ahead! But then something happened that caught me by surprise... some people weren't taking action. What the—?! *Whyyy?!* This led me on the most fascinating journey to discover what makes some people move and other people freeze. It *fascinated* me. Turns out, there was a whole lot more to success than my naive self ever could have imagined. I've spent years unwinding and untangling the false beliefs and self-imposed limitations of entrepreneurs, and I'm excited to reveal much of what I've learned.

One of the biggest takeaways I think you're going to get from this book is that there's a lot that you already know. As you're reading, when you find something that really resonates with you, take it as a sign that your instincts are strong. Too often we shortchange ourselves and let doubt take over. So allow these moments of resonance to be a sign that you're on the right track and commit to following those instincts from now on.

I don't think it's a mistake that you picked up this book. I believe there's something inside you that has been calling and leading you to greater things. Somewhere inside, under the doubt and fear that maybe was handed to you as a child, you know it's there. Whoever told you that you weren't smart enough... they were wrong. Whoever told you that you weren't good enough... they were wrong. Whoever told you that you were *extra*, that you couldn't have nice things or that your dreams were too big... *wrong, wrong, wrong*. Anyone who has ever accomplished anything in this world has a story of overcoming obstacles, and you are writing your story *right now*!

I believe we are all capable of achieving whatever dreams we have for ourselves and more, and I want to do whatever I can to hold your hand and show you—through stories, examples, and tangible exercises—how to unlock that greatness within you. You have a light so bright that it's *bursting* to get out! I believe that it is not only our right as humans, but it is our *responsibility* to shine our light and share our gifts as brightly as we possibly can. The world needs what only we can give. You need my gifts, and I need yours. Together we are unstoppable, and we can change the world, sister!

I've personally watched thousands of women with little to no self-confidence suddenly *decide* to believe in themselves, to act, to follow the advice in these pages—to be messy and unsure in the beginning, but to do it anyway. Learning as they grow. They changed their lives and the lives of their families forever. It is the most amazing thing to see, and I have had the privilege of having a front-row seat for the last several years. I want a front-row seat at your discovery too! Playing it small is so "last year." Time to shine, baby!

It is my intention and heartfelt belief that by the end of this book, you are going to feel a fire within you, reminding you of everything that you already knew deep down—that you are a powerful, fierce, loving, incredible soul who has a purpose, and you will not be able to stop yourself from fulfilling that purpose. You will have clarity and confidence that you can achieve whatever goal you set for yourself—and that *you* are all you need. You won't need acceptance or permission from anyone outside yourself because your belief in your mission will be that *strong*. I know that's a tall order, but that's *my* belief, and nothing outside of *me* will change that. You are amazing and talented, and it's time to get started. You ready? Let's do this!

XO, SHARI

P.S. I feel like I need to tell you that expressing myself without the use of emojis and gifs wasn't easy! #butIstillhavehashtags

PART ONE

The Mindset

Your Growth
Starts Here

1

What Makes You Weird Is Your Greatest Gift

You know, sometimes all you need is twenty seconds of insane courage. Just literally twenty seconds of just embarrassing bravery. And I promise you, something great will come of it.
BENJAMIN MEE, *We Bought a Zoo*

HAVE YOU ever felt out of place, different from everyone else, like you didn't belong, or as if something were wrong with you? Yeah, me too. The first thing you need to know is that in business and in life, it is your uniqueness that will help you stand out and succeed!

Honestly, I don't think I've ever met anyone who didn't feel like a square peg in a round hole at some point in their life. *Hello, middle school!* When we're young, we want to be like everybody else because there is safety in that. Same hair, same clothes, same everything. Flying under the radar helps us avoid being judged or seen as an outsider. To stand out is to risk ridicule, and at times, it's a matter of survival! We strive to keep the spotlight off ourselves for fear of the atomic wedgie or spitballs to the back of the head.

It's not much easier to be our authentic self as we get older, but the tide is turning, and we now live in a culture where everyone is looking for authenticity. People are tired of the surface fluff and are craving the depths that you can only achieve when you are truly yourself. There is nothing better or more liberating than living your life 100% as yourself, expressing the crazy, quirky, wonderful things that make you *you*. It's true freedom! Our personalities are like our fingerprints, completely individual and special. To hold back from living anything other than your 100% authentic, true self is to deprive the world of that special gift that only *you* have to offer!

When I was a kid, I couldn't have been more different than my friends. Every single thing about me was different—my height, my skin color, my hair. All I wanted was to be the same as everyone else, but because I was so glaringly different at 13, being five-foot-ten with freckled, so-pale-I-was-almost-blue skin, and red hair that shined like a beacon, this was not going to be possible. I wanted to find a way to connect and make myself a part of the group, so I had to figure out a way to carve my niche. Turns out humor was my vehicle! Laughter was a tool that I used to feel like I had a place within the group *and* to keep me from being beat up for my differences. #truestory I can't tell you how many times I avoided a butt-whoopin' with a bully because I made them laugh! There was nothing I could do to hide these glaring differences about myself, but looking back, I see that the skills I developed as a kid served me well as I got older. Being different became very familiar, although it was never comfortable.

So let's get one thing straight: We are *all* different in our own way, and this needs to be celebrated! *This* is the secret sauce to success, my friend! The challenge is that we tend to waste so much energy with the false idea that everyone else is special and they all have something that we don't. Once we embrace the things that makes us weird, we are more connected to ourselves and the divine inner wisdom that can guide us. I've seen it time and time again—that what we've been running from and trying to suppress or change in ourselves is *the very thing* that can unlock our greatness. #flythatfreakflaghigh

When I started my network marketing business, I didn't mind stepping out on my own and developing training for my team that was unconventional. For example, when I started selling, I didn't focus on all of the products, just one. The *best* one! People looked at me like I had three heads! (Get in line because people have been looking at me like that since I was a kid.) "Why aren't you focusing on all of the products?!" they would ask me. At the time I knew it was possible that they could be right. But so what? Watch me give it 100% and see what happens. I was loud, I was bold, I was funny. (At least *I* thought so!) Many people told me it wouldn't work, and I was well aware that I could have failed, but again, so what?! I have way more respect for the person who *does* something—who actually makes a move— than the critic sitting on the porch with the puppies! One thing I know about myself is my ability to pivot, and I pivot quickly! If I'm giving something 100% and I start to see a roadblock—I *pivot*! #andnowRossisinyourhead #yourewelcome

Raise your hand—well, not literally because then you'll drop the book, but mentally raise your hand if anyone has ever said any of the following to you:

- Have you ever been told you're "too much"? Well that means you're dynamic. Good for you!

- Are you "too loud"? *Fantastic.* That means you can project and capture an audience!

- Too quiet? Amazing. You're probably a great listener and introspective, which makes you great at strategy!

- Too old? You've got so much experience and wisdom to share!

- Too young? Look at *you* being brave and trying new things at a young age. In ten years you'll be way ahead of the crowd!

In 2015, when I hit that millionaire achievement, the same feelings that I had growing up—of fear, awkwardness, wanting to hide, wanting to blend in—came rushing back. The spotlight was definitely for much better reasons this time around, and I wouldn't have changed that experience for the world, but it was fascinating to me that the feelings were exactly the same! I was

You have the power to decide what thoughts you're going to feed, and it can make all the difference in the world!

afraid of the attention, and I wanted to hide. Can I just have the money and hide under my bed, please?! *Yes*, I was super excited for the achievement—but I didn't really want a big deal made about it because I didn't want the spotlight on me. I freaked out at first and asked the company's owner if he could change the name of the Millionaire's Wall to something that didn't reflect the money. After much consideration they changed the name to the Wall of Influence on the night of my promotion. #whew But that didn't change the fact that I felt a big responsibility to show other women what was possible. The phrase "to whom much is given, much is expected" kept going through my head. It wasn't about me, and it wasn't about my fear or discomfort; it was about the millions of women in the world who needed to know that there was a way to change their circumstances. So I needed to stand loud and proud, even if my knees were knocking. #accidentalleader

To date, more than 400,000 women have joined my team, so I've coached thousands over the last eight years. What I have found time and time again is that every single one of us has our own situations of feeling awkward and different. We all have insecurities, and too often we hide our differences because we compare ourselves to others. "If I could just be more like her, I'd be successful" is a common theme, and I'm here to tell you that it's not true! Right here, right now, I don't care who you are or what your background, *you* can be as successful as you decide to be if you're willing to drop the false beliefs and own what makes you unique! As I coach women on building their online businesses, I am constantly amazed to find these beautiful gems of personality and quirkiness that they've been hiding in their efforts to be like everyone else. *Boring!* Some women have been hiding their unique characteristics for so long that they've forgotten what they were! #bueller #bueller

Comparison Is the Thief of Joy

It's human nature to compare ourselves to our peers. It's how we decide if we are okay. If we are like everyone else, then we feel safe and accepted. This might be okay for adolescents, but we are grown-ass women, and it's time we embrace what makes us magnificent! It is time that we start getting comfortable standing out. The old, tired stories are keeping us stuck, and I'm over it! They are false beliefs, and a belief is just a story we continue to tell ourselves. If we change the story, we change the belief!

I'm sure you've heard this before when it comes to social media: Never compare your behind-the-scenes with someone else's highlight reel. We all know it's true, but boy, is it easy to get sucked into comparison. I've had the great privilege of having a bird's-eye view of thousands of leaders on my team, and I see the stuff that goes on behind closed doors. I've spoken to women who are striving to have a business like "hers" and feel "less than" because the reality of their own business doesn't seem to measure up. And yet if they only knew what was really going on behind the scenes with that other person that they admire so much, they'd most likely feel differently! We all have our struggles. While you may envy a social media influencer for all of her followers and high sales numbers, what you don't know is that she may envy someone else who is building leaders. Her entire business might be based on her sales alone, and she struggles to duplicate and build a team. Most often the biggest challenge of influencers is that other people don't feel like they can measure up to that level of expertise, so they don't even try. Look, we *all* start with zero Facebook friends and Instagram followers. But it's the consistency that builds the numbers. Many influencers go live every day. Is that something you're willing to commit to? Most aren't! I know

I'm not willing to do that, but that's my personal choice. So I give *huge* props to those who do it. It's a balancing act of asking yourself, "What are you willing to do to get the results you desire?" If you're not willing to put in the effort, don't complain about the results you're *not* getting. #youtgottawerk

Those of you who follow me on social media know I'm a straight shooter, so I'm not going to pretend that comparison hasn't affected me! It's funny looking back because I didn't have any comparison issues in the *beginning* of my business. I was so busy building my network and selling that I didn't really notice or care what anyone else was doing because it didn't affect me and my customers. Let me tell you, *that* is the place you want to be in your business! Be so busy and focused on *your* business that you don't have the time or energy to care about what anyone else is doing! I say it all the time—run *your* race! Think of horses on a racetrack with blinders on. They wear those blinders to prevent them from looking to see what the other horses are doing. In order to be the fastest they can be, they focus straight ahead and run their race! Remember, another person's success isn't your failure! See them as an example of what is possible. If you like what you see, look at it as something to aspire to and work toward. Know that you have your own special recipe, and everyone's success will look different.

My biggest comparison hit me a few years into my business. I was one of many top leaders in the company and always looking to see where I could improve. I would say I had a healthy competition with some other leaders in that they were my friends, and I wished them the best, but it was also nice to have something to strive for and something that pushed me to be better. My business was most similar to a leader named Ann, and we would shuffle back and forth; sometimes I was ahead in the leaderboards, and sometimes she was in the lead. Quite often, she was in the lead! *Dang it!* When I was lagging behind, albeit by only a spot or two, I would rack my brain trying to figure out where I was going wrong, what more could I do, what strategy was I missing? "Why was her team stronger than mine?" I would feel like I wasn't doing enough. And then one day... she was gone. #whatthe Turns out, all was not what it appeared to be. I had assumed that her numbers represented a healthy organization, but it was a house of cards and it fell apart. #notmyteatospill #butgurrrl And here I was, thinking my business was lacking!

That was a huge smack to the forehead that reminded me to practice what I preach. I always say that comparison is the thief of joy, and that we never know what's going on behind the scenes, and here it was, living proof! *Duh*, Shari. #srsly All of the time I had wasted feeling like I wasn't doing enough, or I could be doing better, instead of just running my own race! *Ugh!* I was so mad at myself for falling into that old trap.

You never know what someone's real story is, so be very mindful about the story you're telling yourself! You have the power to control how you feel about your business at all times. Allowing self-deprecating thoughts that make you feel like a loser in your business will keep you stuck. Choosing thoughts that make you feel good and empowered about your business are what will drive you forward!

When I began coaching Janet, she was fiftysomething and telling herself that she was living in a twentysomething world and didn't fit in. She thought she had nothing to offer because she couldn't "compete" with these young women. These thoughts that she had chosen to accept would have made anyone feel bad and hesitant about launching an online business! It was time to reframe the reality of the situation, so we did some research to show Janet just how many women there were in her age range who needed the products she had to offer. There was a *huge* population, and these women had much larger amounts of disposable income to buy what she was selling! #cha-ching Her age *was* her gift! Women in her age range weren't looking to young women for advice—they needed Janet! The most interesting thing about all of this was that in a split second, when she saw the research, everything changed. She felt lighter; she felt inspired and excited and was eager to get moving, helping as many women as she possibly could! So what *really* changed? It was 100% her perspective and mindset. Nothing physically had happened, but one minute she was depressed and hopeless, and the next she was full of energy and ready to roll. *You* have the power to decide what thoughts you're going to feed, and it can make all of the difference in the world!

Different Is Interesting!

Baskin-Robbins doesn't just sell vanilla ice cream—they have *31* flavors, right?! Variety is intriguing! It's why we look for cars that stand out, clothes that make a statement—it's why we are fascinated by edgy celebrities. Take Lady Gaga, for example. Whether you love her or not, you've gotta respect her talent, bravery, and creativity. Imagine how different her career would look if she only showed up with 50% of herself or tried to be like someone else. If she held back and didn't give her music, her costumes, and her shows *all* that she had to give, she wouldn't be where she is today! The same can be said for anyone at the top of their game.

I'm not telling you anything you don't know, but here's the question: *Why don't we all strive to share our quirks and special talents with the world?* Probably because it's too personal and vulnerable—I get it. But that's where the magic lives! That is where opportunities bloom. You gotta risk it to get the biscuit!

My goal is that by the time you're finished with this book, you'll have a fresh outlook on your business, and you'll be willing to take a chance and use some of the tools you've found here to help you make your move! I know how scary it can be because in writing this book, I'm sharing a lot of personal, vulnerable moments. I could let myself worry about what other people think, *or* I could stay focused on doing what I feel called to do with 100% of my heart. To the critic, I say, "You are not my people, and that's okay. Be blessed on your journey, because right here and right now, I'm talking to *my* people. So talk to *your* people! #canigetanamen

Maggie is a perfect example of someone who has so much to offer, but she was allowing her fear of what others might say to keep her from being her true authentic self at full volume. She was a performer at heart and loved theater, but was always told she was "too much" in her daily life. She was in the habit of hiding her light, which meant she was missing out on all that she could be and do in the world.

As Maggie and I dug in, we uncovered that there were really only a few people in her life who ever told her that she was too much, but those few people meant a lot to her, so she overvalued their opinion. From a young age she took that label of "too much" and interpreted it to mean that something was wrong with her and she needed to change. She couldn't be her authentic self because she got the message that she wasn't acceptable as she was.

Please hear me when I tell you that the story she was told and that she had internalized was complete and total crap. There is *no such thing* as too much! Got it?! If someone is telling you that you're too much of anything, it's because they feel "less than" in the presence of your greatness and power. It's not you—it's them! You tell these people, "If I am too much, go find less." #boomski #takethatJack

Now, I won't lie and tell you that it was an easy process for Maggie, but the truth will set you free, and when she looked at her situation with a fresh perspective, she realized that she

A belief is only a story that you keep repeating.

had been running her life and making decisions based on what only a few people said. She learned to see that those people had insecurities and lived their life from a place of fear. If Maggie stepped out, that would have undercut some of their own excuses for stepping out. Fear loves company!

It's just like crabs in a bucket. Did you know that if you put crabs in a bucket, they will stay there? The crabs who try to crawl out will be dragged back down by the other crabs. In our circles of friends and family, this is such a common thing, but it doesn't have to be this way. Be the cycle breaker and blast your brilliance! Take that thing that you've been told to hide, and put in on full blast! *Especially* if you're in a place in your life where you feel stuck. Blow the doors off, and be who you were born to be—with zero apologies! Other people's opinions belong to them and are always based on their own fears, so don't adopt what doesn't belong to you.

There is a saying that it only takes 30 seconds of courage to do something great, and so 30 seconds at a time, Maggie stepped out on social media as her authentic, glorious self. You can probably guess what happened. She got more views, comments, and responses from people than she'd ever imagined. Conversations began, and she felt more alive and inspired than ever before, which showed in her posts on social media. Maggie was helping more and more people, and this beautiful cycle of giving and receiving propelled her business forward like never before!

False Truths

Back when I was in college, I was incredibly focused on getting a 4.0 grade average. Don't ask me why! Looking back now, it was ridiculous. I mean, who even cares?! I was so stressed out that it was making me physically ill. It got so bad that my parents signed me up for a stress management class offered by our local hospital, and I was so stressed about that class that I cried on the way there *and* on the way home! #backfire #whoseidea-wasthis *Who has time for another class when I have to focus on getting a 4.0?!* I'm not sure that it did much to help my stress (I'm being kind here, because it didn't!), but I did have one great takeaway from that class. Here's what I learned:

False Truth Triangle

A
The situation. Facts.

B
The story you tell
yourself about A.

C
The emotions
created by B.

Picture a triangle. At the top is A, the situation. In the bottom left corner is B, what you tell yourself about the situation. And the bottom right is C, the emotion created because of the story you tell yourself. Taking my obsession with a 4.0 as an example, let's put that at the top point of the triangle as A, the situation. In the bottom left corner is B, what I told myself about my need to get a 4.0. That was a revelation! Turns out, I was telling myself that if I didn't get a 4.0, then I was lazy and would never get a good job after college. So, based on that story or "false truth," at the bottom right of the triangle was C, and the emotions I created were fear and stress!

When I identified the false story I was telling myself, wrote it down, and looked at it, I could see how ridiculous it was. Of *course* I was stressed out! #mysterysolved Who wouldn't be if they thought that a 4.0 was the only path to success and that their life depended on it?! Dissecting that statement, I asked myself to identify the *real* truth. Was I lazy? No way, Jose! I knew I was a hard worker! Were there people out there who got good jobs after college and didn't have a 4.0? Of course! In fact, *most* people don't have a 4.0, and they go on to live happy, productive lives! I had to recreate my B—what I was telling myself about the situation.

Every time I was stressed, I had to consciously say out loud: "What is the story that is causing this emotion?" And then I would say: "If I don't get a 4.0, it means I'm lazy and I won't succeed in life." Followed by: "Is this true? *No!* Most people don't have a 4.0, and they go on to be successful."

I did this over and over and over until the story changed, which led to a change of belief, which led to *relief.*

Here's another simple example. A mom says to her adult daughter, "Call me when you get home." (This is A, the situation.) Adult daughter tells herself that Mom is smothering and overprotective (this is B, the story), so she is frustrated and angry (this emotion is C) with her mom. Someone else may tell themselves the story (B) that their mom loves them and wants to make sure they are okay, so (C) they feel loved and cared for. Whoa! Stories are so powerful, and they drive us! And okay, yes, the above example was me too! I am a very independent person, and feeling smothered is the *worst* for me! But then I had a friend who thought it was so sweet that my mom did that because the story *she* told was that it was such a loving gesture. Ugh. Okay, fine. #sorryMom

So, when it comes to business, your A's are the *facts* about your business, pure data with no emotion. Maybe your team is small and you want it bigger. Maybe sales are low and you want them higher. It's time to ask yourself, "What are my B's? The stories I am telling myself about my business?" Here are a few common ones:

- "I suck at sales."

- "I suck at sponsoring."

- "Nobody wants to buy from me or join my team."

- "I can't do this because I'm not like these other successful people. I have challenges that they don't have."

If you say these things to yourself, then *of course* you're going to feel like crap and depressed about your business. Who wouldn't? Remember, a belief is just a thought that you keep repeating!

Here's the deal: You don't have to build a business. Did you know that? #wthShari #thenwhyamIhere But seriously, if you don't like what you're doing, then stop. But *please* stop making excuses. It's exhausting you and everyone around you. Because for as many people who make the above excuses, I've seen thousands of women with far worse circumstances making it happen anyway. You can have results or you can have excuses, but you can't have both. So do yourself a favor and get really honest with yourself! Do you really want to build a business and have more income? Are you willing to learn? If the answer is yes, then it's time to change your story! It's the only way to move forward in your business.

How could you reframe these stories?

- "I suck at sales" can be reframed as "I've never really learned how to sell. I could read a book, take an online course, or watch some YouTube videos and hone my selling skills."

- "I suck at sponsoring" and "nobody wants to buy from me or join my team" could be reframed as "I don't really talk much about the business publicly. I could talk about it more often on social media and also do some more activities to expand my network and connect with more people."

- "I can't do this because I'm not like these other successful people. I have challenges that they don't have" could be reframed as "Everyone has challenges, and lots of people have overcome more than this, so it's possible if I really want it."

Can you feel the difference in the energy of these statements? One is closed off, and one is open to possibilities. One is heavy, and the other is light. By changing your B's, the stories you're telling yourself, you will change your C's, the emotions you have about your situation. When you change the story, the belief changes, and success follows! #youcandoit

2

From Insecurities to Influence and Impact

When you make your business about yourself, you put the power in other people's hands. When you make it about serving others, you take your power back.

Taking Inventory

Now that you've got a new perspective on your strengths, it's time to discover all the possibilities that are waiting for you! I hope the wheels have started to turn, and you're contemplating all of your unique qualities. Now is the time to tap into just how powerful you are! Let's get started on building that confidence. Confidence is an inside job; it's something you give to yourself!

What would your friends say are your best qualities? What qualities do *you* admire in a person? Let's assess so you can accentuate your best traits and grow in the areas you'd like to develop.

> **HOT TIP!** If you aren't sure what your strengths are just yet, try this! Create a post on social media asking people to describe you in three words or less. Not only will you gain incredible insight into yourself, but that kind of an engagement post will boost your algorithm! #winwin Look for the common words that people use to describe you. Those, my friend, are your strengths! Write them down on a Post-it note, and put it where you can see it often. Let it be a reminder of who you are and why people love you! What could you do to take those qualities and amplify them? What comes naturally to you? Where do you feel ease and flow in your life or business? If you don't know the answers

> to these questions off the top of your head, this is an area of opportunity. It's time to put yourself on your to-do list and find the answers. They are a big piece to unlocking your business success puzzle!

While it's important to be well-rounded in your business and to eventually develop all the pieces of the business pie, don't underestimate the benefit of going all in and pouring 80% of your energy into the things that you naturally do best. Often that 80% overflows into the other areas where you might feel less than stellar. It's always a good idea to work on the areas where we need improvement—just don't do it to the detriment of your gifts and skills! There's a human tendency to focus on what's lacking, but if something about your business *really* lights you up and you *really* excel at it, make lots of time for that!

This topic reminds me so much of Gracie. Gracie was such a sweetheart, and her friends just adored her. She was on the quiet side online and around people she didn't know, but in small groups of close friends, she was dynamite! You could just feel how much she cared about people—it oozed out of her. She was a selling rock star among her close circle, but she couldn't seem to build a team. As we worked together and dug into her business, we realized that her personal circle was just too small to build from, and she needed to expand her network on social media. Here was the problem—while Gracie was amazing in small groups with people whom she knew, out in the Facebook world, she was like a deer caught in the headlights, wide-eyed and frozen.

Now, we could have focused on Gracie's team-building skills, because the goal was to build a business, right? She already had great sales. But that was a pretty big, scary leap for her. So instead we decided that she should put 80% of her energy into what she did well—care for people. Instead of thinking of going live on social media as "trying to sell and build a business," we reframed her mission. Her assignment was to go live every week at the same time and do what she does best! She prepared her topic and pretended that she was talking to her raving fans, helping them solve problems with the products she was offering, just like she would in person, in a FaceTime call, or if she was making a video to send to one of them.

> **HOT TIP!** When going live on social media, there's no need to wait for anyone to hop on! Most people watch the replay anyway. And there's also no need to read the comments until the live is over. In fact, I recommend hiding the comments if you're nervous and new to lives. Know what you want to say, hit the button, and *go*!

Here's what happened for Gracie. She was nervous and a little stiff the first few weeks, but as she practiced, she loosened up. Her personality and genuine care for others started shining through! She was reaching more and more people, she gained regular followers through consistency, and she started feeling comfortable reading the comments during her live. She was building trust with her community! This trust built rapport, and guess what happens when you build trust and rapport with people? They not only buy from you, but some even decide to join you on the journey!

Gracie began building a team, not by diving into the areas where she was lacking, but by turning up the volume in the area where she excelled! And yes, she was scared and self-conscious, and overthinking everything like we all can do. But she leaned on her strengths, knowing where she wanted to go, and she mapped out a plan with baby steps and consistency to make it happen. Remember, this doesn't happen overnight. It takes a plan and then consistently executing that plan!

Figure out where you are so you know where you're going.

Build Confidence with Servant Leadership

When you make it about yourself, you put the power in other people's hands because you are dependent on their opinions of you. When you make the work about serving others, you take your power back!

Servant leadership can mean serving and leading your team, but it can also mean leading your customers and community. I was 43 years old and only about a week into my business when I discovered this, and things shifted for me in the best way!

While I felt blessed to be able to be a stay-at-home mom, living on one income in Southern California was not easy. There was very little left at the end of the month, and I knew lots of women who were in the same boat. Just a week into my business, when I saw that I could share my love of a product and get paid, I realized that I was sitting on a gold mine! It was so simple, and my friends needed to know about it! We always shared couponing tips and bargains, and this was no different. In fact, this felt like a lotto ticket! I couldn't shut up about it. I talked about it at PTA meetings, school pickup, and even at Target! I was making phone calls and emailing, anything I could do to spread the word because I was *convinced* that I had just found the solution to financial suffering. Yes, it felt *that* dramatic! And the moment I shifted from "What's in it for me?" to "How many women can I help?"—that was the moment my business launched into overdrive!

Now, if I was just doing it from a place of "What's in it for me?" I know that I wouldn't have had the courage to be so bold. But because I knew that this business could lighten every family's financial load, I was willing to go out on a limb and talk about it. As crazy as it might sound, I felt like I had a responsibility to share this opportunity, and if it didn't speak to someone, that was completely fine. But I knew I couldn't live with the guilt of knowing about something so amazing and not sharing it with people who just might be praying for an opportunity to present itself.

I realized that to help as many people as possible, I needed to show up and shine as my brightest self! This wasn't easy for me because I had been labeled a "too much" girl in the past, so I had learned to dial it back, making myself small to make others comfortable. But if I truly wanted to help as many women as I possibly could, I was going to have to let that fear go, stop making it about me, and put my brightest self on blast. I would talk to strangers about the business if the topic of finances or financial struggle came up. For instance, if you were near me in the line at Starbucks and mentioned a layoff, how expensive it was to raise kids, whatever, I was all over it!

"Sorry to interrupt, but I couldn't help overhearing, and you sound just like me. I was in that same position a few months ago before I started this job. Here's my card. Check out the website, and if this speaks to you, let me know. I show women every day how to make money from their phone." How bold is *that*?! In my best Monica Geller voice—*"I know!"* I couldn't believe myself! And don't think it was comfortable for me to do that; my heart was pounding, and I was sweating like a sinner in church! But my fear of embarrassment had to take a back seat because I was doing important work, and my conscience wouldn't let me rest if I didn't at least let people know that this option was out there. I had looked for something like this my entire life, and what if someone hadn't told me about it because they were afraid of how *they* would look? Sounds pretty selfish, doesn't it?

I could never have been so bold if it was about me making money and what that person could do for *me* if she joined my team. I would have been too self-conscious! When we make it about ourselves, we put the power in other people's hands

because we are dependent upon their opinion
I focused on how many women I could he
launched into overdrive!

Happiness vs. Fulfillment

I've learned something very interesting and unexpected over
the course of my network marketing career. I truly believe it's
one of the keys to a better quality of life: learn the difference
between happiness and fulfillment. Abraham Hicks says that
the only reason we want something is because we think we will
feel better when we get it, but the opposite is true. To be *truly*
happy, we have to find a way to feel better now, right where
we're at. When we can be content and appreciate where we are,
we attract more things to appreciate! Being satisfied but eager
for more is the goal!

Have you ever worked hard for a promotion in your business, thinking that if you could just reach that next level, you'd
feel like you had made it and be able to relax? "Once I'm past
that next goal, I'll feel better." You've just gotta get that monkey
off your back, right? And what happens? You reach the goal.
Yay!! You're so happy... but a week later, you're back to being
stressed out. "What if I can't maintain the requirements of this
level now? Am I a fraud? Will I ever be able to achieve the next
goal?" So you hustle and hustle to get that carrot, so you can be
happy—and again, a week later, you're scrambling.

In this equation the promotion equals happiness. Which is
great, but almost immediately after you get it, your brain moves
on to the next goal. What a never-ending hamster wheel. Chasing happiness is exhausting!

Fulfillment is much deeper and longer lasting. It's knowing that you helped someone gain the confidence to take her

first selfie, or that you encouraged someone to believe in herself for 30 seconds to message a potential customer. It's not the followers on social media or the public accolades that leave a lasting effect on your confidence. It's the behind-the-scenes stuff that really matters and can feed your soul! When you see the impact you can make by lifting up another person, it changes you. Showing someone how to solve a problem with your product, how to sell, how to grow a team, how to achieve *their* goal—whether it's to be able to take their family out to dinner once a month, buy their child a pair of shoes, or pay their mortgage—this is the meaty stuff. Who have you helped today? What impact are you making in the world, one person at a time? That's what sticks and what confidence is built upon. Fulfillment is focusing on what really matters. It's the satisfaction that comes from knowing that you made a deeper impact on someone. That never goes away!

I remember once working with a woman named Crystal. She *craved* recognition; it was her main motivator. She wanted to be shouted out constantly because it's what made her feel like she had value and worth. The problem is that when you rely on recognition from outside yourself, you're giving your power away. You're dependent on the actions of others to feel good about yourself. I don't know about you, but that feels like a whole lot of work! Recognition from others is amazing, but it falls into the happiness category, not the fulfillment category, because it doesn't last long. It feels great in the moment, but you've got to constantly chase it to feel good. Don't get me wrong—recognition is *amazing*, but it shouldn't be your oxygen. Think of it as the cherry on top!

When we started working together, Crystal said she was exhausted, and I wasn't surprised. All of her power had been given away to other people, and she was depleted. We talked about ways that she could work her business without draining herself. We concluded that focusing all of her energy on servant leadership—both with her customers and with her team—was the way to go. Her own self-focused trek to public glory had to go on the back burner. It was not easy for her to switch gears, and I remember there was a lot of anxiety in the beginning. Crystal realized that her self-worth was tied up in those public accolades from other people. But as she consistently showed up for her customers and her team, reaching out to see what she could do for *them*, she felt a new sense of appreciation and recognition from them that was a lot deeper than a surface pat on the back.

Witnessing the impact she could make on someone's life and their family by helping them earn a car payment, a night out at the movies, or ballet lessons hit Crystal to the core. Her customers were also so appreciative of the personalized care and attention she gave them. It wasn't just about the quick sale; she followed up and wanted to make sure they were taken care of. Crystal had a lot to be proud of, and that pride grew her confidence! That confidence affected how she showed up in the world. She broke her own cycle of chasing attention and realized that when she was contributing to helping others, she received recognition on a level that she never knew was possible. She had made a difference in someone else's life! Nobody could take that feeling away from her. Just like Dorothy in *The Wizard of Oz*, she realized she held the power all along!

I've watched that shift from "What's in it for me?" to "How many people can I help?" take so many businesses to the next level. I'm telling you, creating more fulfillment is where it's at! Fulfillment is solid, enduring. You'll gain your confidence not from the receiving but from the giving!

3

Fear of Regret vs. Fear of Failure

*Blessings don't always show up
looking the way you think they will.
So keep your eyes open!*

The Rocking Chair Test

Trying to live a life with no regrets has been my biggest benchmark for making decisions, and it's led to some incredible things. For some reason I've always been more afraid of regretting what I *didn't do* than being afraid to fail. But I know from experience that simply telling someone to stop being afraid to fail doesn't work. Instead, I've found that it's better to accept fear, make friends with it in a sense, but then redirect it so it works for you! The fear of failure can cause us all to freeze in our tracks, at times. But I have found that if you want to get yourself moving, focus on the fear of *regret* instead! It will get you into action and lead you to more opportunities!

For over 30 years I've used something I call the Rocking Chair Test as a tool for making decisions. I have no idea where I got this idea, but here's how it works. I picture myself in my old age, sitting on my porch in a rocking chair surrounded by grandkids. Then I ask myself, "What great stories will I have to tell? What adventures will I have to share? Am I going to be a boring old lady with nothing fun to reminisce about?" When I'm faced with an opportunity, I ask myself, "Will I look back and regret saying no? Even if I failed, would this be a great story to tell my grandkids?" I found that it's easier to take action when I take the focus off my fear of failure and think about it as an adventure that will make a great story, no matter the outcome.

Stick the Landing!

I remember my very first Rocking Chair Story. I was scared out of my mind but thought, "Worst-case scenario, this will be a great story to tell." And *indeed* it has been. I've gotten a lot of mileage out of my big audition story!

So back in the early '90s, there was a TV show called *In Living Color*, and it had hip-hop dancers called the Fly Girls. One day, as I sat down in my college history class, the girl next to me said, "Hey! Did you hear that there are open auditions for the Fly Girls tomorrow? I know you dance, so you should go!"

Gulp. Adrenaline shot through me like a rocket! Wow! How awesome would that be?! But how terrifying! I had never been to an audition like that and didn't know the first thing about it. But I kept thinking, "What if this is it?! What if this is my big break that God is sending my way? So what if I fail? I've got nothing to lose. If it's meant to be, it will happen, and if not, I've got a great story to tell!"

So off I went, into the big scary city. By the time I found the audition, I could see *hundreds* of young women lined up around the building and down the street for several blocks. I found out on the news later that day that there were over 1,500 women who auditioned!

Now, let me paint this picture for you. I like to call it "Holly Hobbie Goes to Hollywood." (Holly Hobbie was a doll dressed in prairie clothes, in case you're too young to get that reference!) I was wearing tights, a leotard, and a big coat to cover it all. I found myself standing in line behind women with gold sparkly unitards with big holes cut out all down the sides. Everyone was dressed like it was a Vegas showgirl competition, and little hometown me looked like I was dancing for a church picnic. *So* out of place! I hugged my coat closed and pretended I wasn't sticking out like a sore thumb! It's so funny to think back on it all because as I was getting to the front of the line, I noticed that these other women had headshots and résumés. Ha! Whatever for? So funny, I thought! I was a business major, and résumés were only for real jobs. I can't even believe how naive I was. So I asked to borrow a piece of paper, and I wrote down my name and "high school dance team—first-place dance competition winner," like an idiot. #facepalm *Cringeworthy!!* And then I proceeded to go sit and wait to be called in with the bazillions of others. I remember one of the actors on the show, Tommy Davidson, walked by and said, "I hope this place doesn't catch on fire, because every woman in Los Angeles is here right now!"

So the deal was, you wait to be called, you go inside the studio and learn the dance, and then you perform it. While we were waiting outside, there were women climbing on top of each other to peek inside the small windows to see the dance routine so they could learn it early. Being the ultimate rule follower that I was, I felt like this was cheating, so I just sat and waited like I was supposed to. Well... once they called me in with about 20 others, I kid you *not*, they showed us the dance routine three times and then said, "Go." And we had to perform it as a group. *Whaaat?* I was a fast learner but *come on!* I was reconsidering my life choices at that moment, but I thought, "Okay, if that's how it is, let's do this thang!" Let's also ignore the fact that the stars of the show—Keenen Ivory Wayans, Damon Wayans, Jim Carrey, and Rosie Perez—were sitting right there watching. I was trying not to pass out!

So, right as they were about to cue the music, I realized that the lady standing in front of me was too close, and I couldn't back up. I have really long legs, and there was a fan kick coming, so she was at risk of getting a high-top Reebok to the back of the head. I politely asked her if she could scoot up because I was afraid that she would get hit by my flying leg. She was having *none* of it and proceeded to tell me to "eff off." *Alrighty then!*

Well, I'm sure you can guess what happened. The music started, and we were all over that dance floor, trying to keep up and just *remember* the moves. It was a hot mess—well, not so much "it" as "me"—and so embarrassing, but hey, I was there and giving it my all! One thing I always remembered from dance classes was that no matter how badly you screwed up, you should nail the ending like it was the performance of a lifetime! So, we were nearing the end, then the fan kick—and *boom*! Reebok to the back of her head. #killmenow

Aaand it gets worse. The momentum threw her forward, and she landed facedown and slid across the dance floor like she was sliding into home plate. I was *horrified*! But as they say, my friends, the dance goes on, and I had that landing to stick. So at about the time her body came to a halt in front of the cast of the show, I hit that last move like I'd invented it! When I looked up, I could see the cast laughing so hard that they had tears streaming down their faces... well, all but Rosie Perez. She was the choreographer, so she didn't quite get the comedy of it all. Jim Carrey stood up in front of me, extended his arms, and started clapping. Now, we both knew at that moment that I was not destined to be a Fly Girl, but I believe he appreciated my comedic timing and that I gave it my all! #thestoriesItellmyselftoeasethepain Let's just say I grabbed my coat and ran to my car as fast as I could. #middleschoolbuttwhoopinflashbacks

So, let's unpack this situation. I took a chance, I put myself out there in a very public way, I embarrassed myself, I "failed"... and so what?

- Did I die?
- Did I learn?
- Did I gain experience?
- Was I proud of myself for trying?
- Do I have a great story?
- Was I brave?

Except for the "die" part, that's a big *yes* to all of the above! #didnotdie #justtobeclear And now I don't ever have to wonder

Finish strong! You may not know what you're doing, but that's okay. **Do it anyway! You won't regret it!**

"What if?" What if that was meant to be my big break, and I had missed it because I was too afraid? What if that experience led me to another experience, and another, and eventually I found my path and purpose? I don't have to live with any of those thoughts because I *did* explore the opportunity, and now I have a hilarious story to tell. And I have something to use as a teaching tool to show that taking risks and seizing opportunities are what life is about, even when they make us nervous! How can something amazing happen if we don't step outside our comfort zone? So stop worrying so much about failing. Be brave! Go out there and do something that is going to give you a great Rocking Chair Story!

Don't Judge That Blessing by Its Cover

I'm always fascinated to look at life in the rearview mirror and recognize how many blessings wouldn't have happened if it hadn't been for a seemingly "bad" experience. My divorce was a perfect example of this. I married my high school sweetheart after I graduated from college, and after being together for over 11 years, we were married for only six months. It wasn't his fault. He just forgot to stop dating. It happens. #blesshisheart #sarcasm

I can laugh about it now, but at the time it was a complete and total implosion of my life! I was running into people at the grocery store whom I hadn't seen since the wedding. They'd congratulate me on my marriage, and I'd break down into a heaping, bawling mess right there in the frozen-food aisle. It was heartbreaking and humiliating, and not to sound dramatic, but it felt like those 11 years of my life had been a lie. It had been almost half of my life! I didn't even know who I was without him. Looking back, I see why that betrayal and divorce was the absolute best and most important thing to ever happen for my personal development! I mean, I'm throwing years of anguish into a tiny nutshell here, but I can honestly say that I wouldn't be who I am today and have the perspective that I do if it wasn't for the experience of the divorce. Now, please understand that it took me a long time to see the full blessing in all of it. I mean sure, we didn't have kids, and nobody wants to be married to someone they can't trust, so that revelation was immediate. But the deeper stuff sank in down the road.

When you experience something that rocks you to your core, there can be an incredible silver lining. It shows you that you're stronger than you ever thought possible. Very little scares you after you get through it! You learn to keep your eyes open and pay attention to the signs when they are still little. There's a saying, "God guides us with feathers, and when we don't listen, he throws bricks." Lol. I don't want any more bricks. #thankyouverymuch As much as that experience wrecked my confidence, coming out on the other side of it is what *built* my confidence! I didn't need anyone but myself. I wasn't going to settle for anything less than what I deserved. I had the opportunity to choose again, and to choose wisely this time.

I obviously had trust issues in the beginning! #moreissuesthanVogue But then I realized that the only person I had to trust was myself. I trusted that no matter what anyone threw at me, no matter what decisions another person made, I could take care of myself and be okay. The freedom of this realization was life-changing. I have zero control over what another person does anyway, so accepting that and letting go was such a gift. It was one of those situations where, as painful as it was, I wouldn't have changed a thing. I needed to go through it so that I could realize how strong I was, and that confidence helped me become who I am today.

This lesson didn't just apply to personal relationships; it also applied to being self-employed! It's where I learned resilience and how to remain calm when business isn't going the way I think it should go. It's where I learned not to freak out because the sales numbers, *or* the product, *or* the back order, *or* the out-of-stock items weren't matching the picture I had in my head. I learned that everything works itself out, and if I can remain calm and clearheaded, the process is much less dramatic. Remember, don't discount the painful stuff; it's where you uncover the best parts of yourself and often find your biggest blessings!

GINA CAME to me for coaching because she had been wanting to build a team and really make her business work. She said she had been praying for a business where she could help other women, but so far, she had only recruited a few people, and she was thinking of quitting. Gina told me that a year ago a woman named Ava had joined her team. Ava started out like gangbusters with her sales and built a small team, but within six months, she stopped working. She wouldn't return Gina's messages and basically just disappeared. I call that going into the Witness Protection Program, and listen, it happens to all of us! #hello #anyoneoutthere So my first question to Gina was, "Why are you basing your business decisions on what another person is doing, or not doing, with her business?" Gina was under the impression that the people on Ava's team belonged to Ava, and so Gina had never reached out or built a relationship with them. She felt like she would be stepping on Ava's toes, so to speak. Listen closely when I say this—*no*. The end. Got it? Nobody "belongs" to anyone.

> **HOT TIP!** In this business we are independent contractors, and in my opinion, we have an obligation to connect with the people on our team, no matter who they joined under. Why wouldn't someone want to have as much support as they possibly could?

Gina had assumed that if Ava stopped working, the entire team was lost to her. Not necessarily! Those people joined for a reason—so find out the reason. Listen, if you recruit someone who recruits a few people and then they disengage from the business, *scoop that team up*! What a blessing! You just gained teammates whom you never would have had without them, so go introduce yourself. Those teammates have *hundreds* of contacts each, so help them tap into that network! Even if they decide they don't want to work the business, treat them like your VIP customers and get referrals. Get to know their circle of friends; perhaps offer an online class or party.

What Gina thought was a business-ending situation turned out to be a huge blessing. Some of those women whom she dreamed of helping were right under her nose all along. I'm happy to report that when she reached out to the team, she found many who were so happy to have someone to work with and mentor them! They had been feeling lost themselves because they didn't feel like they had anyone to go to for help. Gina learned an important lesson that changed the way she worked her business from that day forward.

Moral of the story: *Do not* make decisions or assumptions about your business based on what someone else *is* or *is not* doing! You are the captain of your ship; you have all the power, so decide what *you* want to do. Period. And realize that blessings are often right under your nose, but they just may not be wrapped up with the cute little bow you imagine. I always remind myself that I can't pray for guidance and then ignore it when it shows up because it doesn't look the way I think it should. I feel like the guidance will stop coming if I don't pay attention and act!

4

Everything Is Always Working Out for You

*You'll never see the solution
if you're wallowing in the problem.*

F YOU'VE followed me on social media, you've heard me use the phrase "everything is always working out for me" over and over! This is one of my favorite mantras, and I repeat it as often as I can because the more I repeat it, the more I believe it, and as a result, the more evidence I receive that it's true! It makes my life more peaceful and joyful, and I witness miracles on a regular basis. I would also initially use this phrase to calm myself down when something that I did *not* want to happen happened. So maybe I was a bit sarcastic about it in the beginning, saying it with an eye roll, but I realized that when I started looking for ways in which things *were* working out for me, more positive things started showing up! It's like when you're shopping for a particular car and suddenly you see that car everywhere. Or when you're wanting to have a baby, and suddenly it seems that the whole world is pregnant! Thoughts become things, and we get what we think about—whether it's wanted or not.

Bless This Mess!

I won't pretend and tell you that I've *always* felt like things were always working out for me. Ha! Not even close! For much of my life, I felt like I was lost and wandering around aimlessly. It wasn't until I was in my forties that I could look back

Even when bad things happen, if you keep an attitude that the universe is conspiring on your behalf, **you can turn things around and bounce back faster.**

on my life and see the blessings in my struggles. When I went through my divorce, I would tell myself that everything happens for a reason, just to keep myself from falling into a deep, dark depression. On some level I believed it, but it didn't stop the pain. It was about two years later that I realized I wouldn't have changed that experience for anything. I never realized how strong I was until being strong was my only choice. When you go through your biggest fear, there's very little you're afraid of after that! It taught me so much, and I came to terms with the fact that I am not what has happened to me; it was simply an experience I had that made me stronger.

Being divorced at 24 is pretty embarrassing. Being cheated on adds to the humiliation. But I knew I was a lot more than that experience. At the very least, this was going to make a great Rocking Chair Story, right?! #mygrandkidsareinforarealtreat

I LOVE this analogy—imagine yourself as a lighthouse, and the experiences you're having are like the storms that blow past you. They can be rough and dramatic; you might be bruised and have some scars, but you're still standing! You're strong because you survived the storm, and sunny days are on the way! It's so very important to avoid falling into victim mode, as justified as it might be, because victim mode is like quicksand. Once you get stuck, it's hard to get out and move forward. Get into survivor mode and take your power back!

Over the years, I have looked back on that divorce and been so incredibly grateful that it happened. Without it, I wouldn't have the life I have now, and I feel like it also prepared me for the miscarriages I had years later. (Yes, my life could be several episodes of *Oprah*!) It might sound strange, but when I was going through miscarriage after miscarriage (five total and four within one year), I thought back to what my divorce taught me. I learned that I was strong, that this feeling wasn't going to last forever, and most importantly, that these were just experiences I was having. It was an incredibly hard time! I was devastated, depressed, and scared. Even though I knew that in the *big* picture things would be okay, it was still a difficult journey. But I kept the faith that there were reasons this was happening that I couldn't see yet.

You might be wondering how on Earth "everything was always working out for me" when I was experiencing so much loss. In retrospect, I can see that I needed more time between the birth of my daughter and my son. Little did I know at the time that my son was going to be a challenging child, and if my kids were closer than three years in age... well, I quiver at the thought! Mama might not have survived that without a team for mental and emotional support! But once again, these tough circumstances showed me how strong I was, that I could do hard things, and I did end up having another healthy baby. #hallelujah

Lessons on Leadership

I don't care who you are or where you're from; we all deal with difficult people, many of whom want to tear us down from time to time. I'm definitely no exception. Within the first year of growing my business, I noticed that a couple of women on my team began acting strange. They were distant, not returning messages, and it made no sense to me at the time. Nothing had happened; there hadn't been any disagreements, but I started hearing through the grapevine that they were talking badly about me to their teams. As much as I wanted to confront it head-on and set the record straight, I knew that would become a huge distraction. I also knew that the truth would come out eventually—because it always does—so my best and smartest course of action was to continue to be myself, maintain my integrity, and work my business. It was hurtful, frustrating, and confusing to see grown women behaving in such childish ways, telling lies and trying to tear me down. But as difficult as it was, I knew that this pettiness didn't matter in the big scheme of things. My pride wanted me to kick some ass, but my business brain knew I had bigger fish to fry! Just like the advice I gave Gina (back in chapter 3), I wasn't going to let someone else's behavior determine what actions I take in my business. And now, six years down the road, I have absolute clarity and confirmation that these women and their antics didn't matter. Considering my eight-year career in network marketing, this situation was like a gnat flying around my head. We all have gnats, and we always will. We also have the power to decide what we allow to distract us! #squashthatbug

I had an important "aha moment" during this challenging situation—I realized that while I was the type who rarely had any drama or conflict with others, these women had conflict with people *all the time*. It was a regular part of their lives! They were the only people in my life whom *I* had issues with, but I was one of *many* that they had issues with. So remember that people behave badly because of what's going on inside *them*, not because of you. Their behavior is a reflection of them and only them!

If you find yourself in the middle of drama, my best advice is to put your head down and focus on your business! Ignore the haters—because they don't matter. It's a phase in your career that will teach you important lessons, and the experience will enable you to help your team when they go through it—and they *will* go through it, because we all do!

I know it's easy to become emotional when things feel personal, but when it comes to your career and livelihood, you need to put your business hat on. Like Don Miguel Ruiz says in one of my favorite books, *The Four Agreements*, "Don't take anything personally." I know a lot of you are thinking, "Shari, how can I not take it personally when they are making it personal?!" Listen, hurt people hurt people. It's them, not you! If you allow yourself to be like a pinball, bouncing around because of what someone else says or does, you give them all your power. Stay focused on your goals! And remember, no experience is wasted. Going through challenges makes you a better leader. If everything was supersmooth all of the time, you wouldn't be able to relate to the struggles your team might be having, and so you wouldn't know how to guide them. The challenges are what make you a great leader and businesswoman, not the easy times!

Bottom line? Blessings aren't always obvious in the moment, and it's not until we look back in hindsight that we can see how everything worked out for us. I'm asking you to become more aware in those tough times, and the minute something happens that scares you ... take a breath and remind yourself that everything *is* always working out for you, and expect to see the silver lining. It's there! The sooner you look for it, the sooner you'll find it!

Here's a great exercise: Set a timer and spend at least five minutes imagining your future. When you are five years down the road and enjoying the rewards for all of your hard work— ask yourself if any of the current situations that are annoying you will matter. Nine out of ten times the answer is *no*! They will be a blip on your radar, an inconsequential nuisance, and the sooner you ignore them and get focused on the business at hand, the faster you will move forward! #giddyup

Are You Living in the Problem or the Solution?

The best leaders are the ones who have been through the most crap. Think about it: Would you rather have a leader who has had nothing but smooth sailing in her career or one who has been down in the trenches, knows exactly what you're going through, and has come out the other side? I mean, don't make me give you a *duh*! When you're going through some rough stuff, it's your classroom; it's your education! Entrepreneurship is 100% on-the-job training, so don't be resistant to experiences that may seem "bad." There is something to be learned in every situation, and nothing lasts forever, so hang tight, buttercup! #herecomesthesun #doodoodoodoo

One of the scariest situations in my career actually ended up launching my business into the stratosphere! Mascara was our hero product. It was so good that it practically sold itself, so that's all we focused on. We were in hyper growth and selling massive amounts; people were joining the company left and right and then... it went on back order—for six weeks! *Ummm... okay... sooo, now what?* People were freaking out, crying, and even quitting!

Sidebar: If you're new to sales and entrepreneurship, let me tell you that *spit* happens. I've been in retail sales and management, wholesale and outside sales, and self-employed, and there is *always* something. Always. Always. Erryday. Get used to it. #bigwhoop Even if you're not from a sales background, have you ever had any sort of work done on your house? Or your car? Something is always delayed or back-ordered, a part is out of stock, yada, yada, yada. It's maddening, but it's life!

Anyhow, at that point, amidst all of the wailing, moaning, and gnashing of teeth, my team of over 2,000 people were all looking to me. Mind you, I had been in the business for only about six months, but if I wanted to have a business in the *coming* six months, I had to do something, and fast! While having such a big team was awesome, it was also a big responsibility, so don't fool yourself into thinking it was all hearts and rainbow ponies! Since I had no power over a back order, the only thing I could control was my perspective and my attitude.

Here's the pivot that changed everything: Instead of telling the story that our number-one product was out of stock, so we couldn't sell anything, the story became, "Our product is *so good* that it went viral and sold out! Place your order for this amazing stuff *today* because when it comes back, the mascara orders will be shipped in the order they are received, so get in line ASAP!" *Boom.* Seriously, in two seconds our business tripled, and the only thing that changed was our mindset and messaging. Women began promoting at the speed of light, and I—along with dozens of others—hit the top of the company during this back order! In hindsight that back order put us on the map. What appeared to be this horrible situation ended up being the best thing that ever happened to us!

I still marvel at the fact that nothing *actually* changed except how everyone viewed the situation. It's fascinating to see how in a split second, things can change, but that change is always internal. The facts of the situation remained the same, and yet ... one minute women were hopeless and crying, and the next they were empowered and enthusiastic! Remember our False Truth Triangle from chapter 1? A is the situation, B is what we tell ourselves about the situation, and C is how we feel because of what we tell ourselves. Yes, we have that much power over our circumstances, but not if we sit in the suck! #nosucksitting

If you want to wallow and fight for your limitations, well, sister, I'm gonna let you. I've exhausted myself trying to drag people across the finish line, and that experience has taught me that it doesn't work long-term. We all tend to drag people in the

When you wallow
in the problem,
**you can't see the
solution.**

beginning, thinking that's what a good leader or mentor does. Let me save you the time and energy by saying... *nope*. When you get yourself over that finish line, holler back and say, "Who wants to cross? I can help! Here's how I did it!" Those who step up and get themselves across the finish line are your people. I mean, still love the ones who stay seated. Love them where they're at! But don't worry more about them and their business than they do. Work with the willing! Anyone who requires dragging will just drown you both, eventually. Once you stop pulling them, they are going to stop anyway, so just save yourself and be the lighthouse! A lighthouse doesn't run all over the island saving boats. A lighthouse remains still, shining its light!

I think about the people who wallowed in the pain and the fear of the back order, but after a few weeks of that, where did it get them? It completely stopped their progress and stalled their business. Those of us who were solution-minded pulled ourselves out of the ditch of despair and made it happen. We took what appeared to be a business-ending situation, created momentum and excitement, and sold even *more* during the back order than we ever would have had the product stayed in stock. #booyababy #everythingisalwaysworkingout

Some people couldn't, or *wouldn't*, get themselves out of the problem mindset, and so they tried to complain louder and louder, but look, what are you gonna do? It's out of your hands! So the sooner you accept that which you *cannot* control and focus on the solution by taking action on what you *can* control, the sooner you get yourself out of the ditch. Don't let the ditch-diggers drag you down!

Misery does indeed love company, so be mindful of the people you surround yourself with. You cannot get sad enough to make someone else happy, so give it up. I used to kill myself trying to convince people to drop their negativity and look to the solutions, but I gave that up too. I'm here talking about solutions and finding the opportunities in challenges. If you want to run with me, let's do it! If you want to continue to beat the dead horse of the problem, I'm going to let you, but I'm not going to listen. You know where I'll be when you get tired of that. I'll be over here hanging with the problem solvers, the dreamers, and the doers—the people who feel like sunshine! These are the people who are forward focused, and they will find solutions.

That back order was a hard couple of months, keeping ourselves above the negativity and focused on the solution. It was too difficult for many, but those who had the right mindset and knew that it wasn't going to last forever thrived and reaped incredible rewards! Once everything calmed down, I heard from many who left that they wished they had stuck it out. This is why mindset is *the* most important thing in any business. What you tell yourself is literally everything. Stamina, persistence, consistency, positivity, and hope are the foundations of success!

One of the *biggest* reasons to move into solution mode as soon as possible is not just because it's best for your business—it's best for *you*. Emotionally, mentally, and physically! #Imtalkingtoyou #youknowwhoyouare You will wear yourself *smooth out* if you stay in the problem mode—because there will *always* be problems.

I once worked with an amazing leader named Jaymie. She was fantastic, but she was burning herself out on every level. Everything to Jaymie was a level ten! Overreactors Anonymous, here she comes! She was super passionate about her business, which was great, but no matter what the issue, big or small, she took everything to heart and acted as though the sky were falling. She told herself the story that a good leader takes on everyone's concerns and fears, and is responsible for making everyone on her team happy. #uhoh She thought there should be zero problems. *Ummm* . . . this false story will kill you. Just sayin'. Not only is it *not true*, but it is toxic and detrimental to your health, your growth, and your overall well-being.

Jaymie told me, "Oh don't worry. My team doesn't know how I feel; I only tell you." If I've heard this once, I've heard it a thousand times, and I'm here to tell you that your vibe is your vibe, baby! Have you ever seen someone smile, but you could tell her heart wasn't in it? People know when you're faking it. They can spot the difference between heartfelt enthusiasm and when there's an underlying fear or concern. *Nobody* is that good of an actor, and even if you are, according to the law of attraction, your vibe or frequency will attract things that match it. Nervous Nelly will attract more nervous Nellies and things to be nervous about. Eeeks! Who wants that?! *Stop it!* Better than faking it, how about you find ways to eliminate it? #yesplease

Let's get a few things straight:

1   You are *not* responsible for the happiness of your team. You are responsible for showing them how to sell and how to build a team of their own. Their emotional IQ, also known as EQ, is their responsibility.

2   You are *not* a support agent. Your corporate office supplies those, so send your people to the corporate website. This isn't you being unsupportive—this is you teaching these self-employed entrepreneurs where to find answers so they can show *their* teams where to find answers. The more time you spend as a support agent to your team, the less time you have to help them grow a business and to grow your own!

3   A calm leader instills calm into her team. Being calm and positive in a crisis isn't insensitive or naive—it's leadership.

4   There will always be problems. (Someone slap that phrase on a T-shirt!) Figure out what you can control and drop what you can't.

All of the above are much easier said than done. I know because I struggled, doing the wrong things. Learn from my mistakes! You do not have to sacrifice yourself to have a strong and healthy team and business! Become an expert at identifying what you can control as quickly as possible. When something is out of your control, focus your team on something productive until the situation resolves itself. As with the "Great Back Order Debacle" that I described above, opportunity lives in those times of uncertainty. So many times, I've seen a distraction lead to new insights and better ways to work the business!

Remember, energy flows where your focus goes. So as much as you may want to beat a dead horse and go on and on about your problems, to grow you need to pivot ASAP and move past the hurdles. The more we talk about a subject, the more energy we give to it—keeping it alive. Pay attention to what you're giving life to. Starve the things you don't want in your business! Talk about solutions, not problems, because isn't that really what you want? Everything has a solution, so put yourself in that frame of mind and watch what happens!

5

You Win
or You Learn

Everyone makes mistakes,
and the most successful people
make the most mistakes!

Pivot to Prosper

Have you ever noticed that when you watch an awards show and someone receives a big award, they always talk about how they came from humble beginnings and the odds were stacked against them? Every. Single. Time. I've never heard an acceptance speech where the recipient mentioned having lots of money to start with and all of the support in the world, and how everything was so simple and easy. It rarely, if ever, "just happened." They tell stories of seemingly insurmountable odds and how they were told "no" repeatedly, or told that they didn't have what it takes, and yet there they were—because they didn't give up. They figured out a way to make it happen *in spite of* the odds! Those who make their dreams come true aren't lucky. Luck happens when preparation meets opportunity, so as long as you continue to prepare and expect to find an opportunity, that opportunity will show up!

As I was growing my team, I was so eager to inspire where I could, and let's just say I "learned" a lot. Also known as "I made a lot of mistakes." One stands out to me, and I'm so grateful for it because it changed how I ran my business and how I coached.

I've always loved doing incentives and creating selling challenges for my team just to keep things fun. I find that whenever I can turn something into a game, I get more accomplished and have a better time doing it! As my income increased, the value of the prizes I offered increased to include Coach bags and wallets, Kate Spade sunglasses, and all sorts of cool stuff that came because of a big paycheck and living near an outlet mall. Sounds great, right? I didn't see anything wrong with it—I was just sharing the wealth, so to speak. As women on my team were promoting to leadership levels and going off to create their own online team training groups—which is what they should be doing—they were telling me that their people didn't want to leave my team page because I had such great prizes. My brand-new leaders were feeling defeated and undermined, and didn't know how they would ever lead a team of their own if they couldn't even get them into their team training groups. Yikes! This was *not* my intention! #facepalm

Once I realized what was happening and what I'd done, I made a quick pivot. I kept the fun incentives, but I made sure they were duplicatable! For example, the first week's incentive would be a small item from our line of products that I could purchase with product credit. Anyone could earn product credit in our company, so the incentive was completely duplicatable. As the month progressed, the prize values increased slightly. Nobody even mentioned the shift in prizes, which shocked me! I realized that the team just liked the game of it all. It was fun to win a prize, no matter what it was! Keep this in mind if you're doing any sort of team incentives, and use whatever your company offers so that it can be duplicated.

This is a great time to remind you that building a network marketing business should *not* cost you any money. The whole concept of "you've got to spend money to make money" does not apply here. That's the beauty of this business! When I see people talk about how they couldn't make money in network marketing, it just shows me that they didn't know how to sell or how to run a business, and they weren't interested in learning. Learning is free with the Internet! Anyone can make money selling products online if they are willing to read a book or just Google it. #doyourresearch

When the team started to see that their leaders were offering the same incentives I was offering, they were more receptive to branching out and following their leaders. In fact, they were excited to move on because the team sizes were smaller, so the odds of winning increased! One of the great silver linings of my mistake was that my new leaders got to see first-hand that when we do our best and sometimes it doesn't work out, we can quickly pivot to correct the issue. We are all a work in progress and learning as we go! Even with the best of intentions, we are all going to screw up, but so what? It's your willingness to learn and pivot that matters.

> **HOT TIP!** The goal is to train people on how to work the business and become leaders and then get those little birds out of the nest! That's duplication. You don't want to grow a team that constantly depends on you. I mean, it's great for the ego, but it's bad for the business. As they say, your ego is not your amigo!

If It Weren't for Bad Luck, I'd Have No Luck at All!

This is a phrase that my friend Carrie used to say all the time. It's also a country song, and *man*, I need an emoji here so badly, it hurts! Lol. #helpme For years, Carrie always felt like she was taking one step forward and four steps back in her business. She would achieve a promotion but then wouldn't be able to maintain it, except for maybe twice a year during big sales months. Has this every happened to you? If not, it most likely will. It's just part of the selling game, so don't take it personally. The higher up you go in your organization, the bigger your team will be and the more moving parts you'll have. So it may take you a bit to get your business to the point where you are maintaining that higher level, month after month.

For example, it is completely normal to hit a promotion during a big month like November and then not be able to hit that level again until the following November. You might find yourself back to those large numbers in a booming spring month and then again the following November, but if you are beating yourself up because you can't "measure up" to that gigantic month the rest of the year, well... I can't help you, because I can't cure normal. It is *normal*. If you hit a promotion in a month like November, that's *fantastic*! But those giant sales numbers only happen once, *maybe* twice, per year.

If you keep doing the work, growing and building, you will get there! The key is not to allow yourself to become distracted and depressed because you're not seeing those large numbers. The secret is that you don't stop selling, looking for new customers, seeking referrals, and talking to people interested in building a business—*because this is the job!* If you stop to look at where you are, you won't ever get where you're going. If you have *time* to stop to look and worry about where you are, you've got time on your hands that you could be putting into your business and doing the things that move the needle!

Pop quiz: How do you know when you're ready for your next promotion? When you're halfway to your goal two or three weeks into the month! This may sound annoyingly obvious, but you'd be surprised how many people say they are "pushing" for a promotion, and two weeks into the month, they are only a tenth of the way there. Be careful, because if you push too hard, you're going to burn out your team and yourself! Instead, see if you can get halfway to the goal by the 15th of the month. Even if you can get halfway to the goal by the third week of the month, quite often it's possible to pull out half of the entire month's sales volume in that last seven to ten days of the month because your team is awake and focused!

Carrie hadn't been able to recreate the same amount of business in the months following her November promotion, and she was telling herself the story that she was a fraud. (She wasn't.) She told herself that her business was going backwards. (It wasn't.) I'm sure you can see how this story was wearing her down. Her confidence was shaken, she was fearful, and that led to tremendous stress. Burnout wasn't far behind! When we took another look at her situation and the story she was telling herself, we dug for a new perspective. We checked her assumptions and expectations, and created a new narrative. This is the story we came up with:

> Carrie had an incredible month in November because of the preparation and growth she and her team had in the previous year. Her month was so great that she hit a promotion! Of course, sales in the following months weren't as big as November, but Carrie and her team were focused on making the most of the new customers they had gained. In the months that followed, business wasn't as hectic from a sales perspective, so the team was taking advantage of that extra time and working closer with their new customers to provide great service. They followed up regularly and built rapport. Each new customer was a doorway to hundreds of new referrals!

Now, doesn't *that* sound fantastic?! Can you feel how different that is from the previous story of fear and lack? *And* it is truer than the initial story she was telling herself. One story is draining, and one story is energizing! We removed the drama. I mean, unless you're filming *The Real Housewives of Network Marketing,* save the drama for your mama!

The best part about all of this is that the new story lifted a weight off of Carrie's shoulders and got her back into action.

Ups and downs, highs
and lows—they're all a part of
being human and especially
being an entrepreneur. **Develop
thick skin and become
obsessively positive!**

Once again, nothing had *actually* changed except her perception of the situation. What felt like a dark cloud over her head gave way to a few rays of sunshine and possibilities! It's not about lying to yourself; it's about putting your business hat on, removing the emotion from the situation, and looking at the facts. Telling a story that gets you back into *action* is the goal!

Ask yourself if your story is more about your weaknesses or more about your strengths. Do you talk more about what you think you *can't* do or more about what is possible? Most people talk more often about what they can't do and why they can't do it than they talk about their possibilities. You're going to get what you think and talk about the most, so when you beat the drum of what you don't want, what do you think you're going to get? *Bingo!* More of what you don't want! So let's stop that, k? K.

Let your story be about your strengths! What are you good at? What do you love? If you put 90% of your energy into the things that you're good at and that come easy to you, instead of 90% of your time worrying about what you're lacking, you will see results! Spend that extra 10% of your time and energy reading a book or taking a course to educate yourself on what you feel you're lacking. I've seen time and time again that the people who have the most "skills" aren't the ones who have the most success—it's the ones who do it, do it scared, do it even when it's not perfect, but have great enthusiasm and consistency. Focus on your strengths!

Jack of All Trades, Master of None

Have you ever heard the phrase "Jack of all trades, master of none"? Essentially it means you can do a lot of different things pretty well, but there isn't one thing in particular that you're really great at. *Ha!* Story of my life! (Insert eye roll here!) For a pretty big chunk of my life, I was changing jobs every two years. Either the hours no longer worked with my college schedule, or I would get bored, or I would be at the point where I just couldn't take one more day of it! There always seemed to be something not quite right. I just couldn't find a job that fit, and that left me feeling lost well into my mid-thirties. I was searching for my niche, my purpose, and all I seemed to find were odd jobs. I felt like I was wasting my time, like I had no direction, and I wondered where I had gone wrong. Maybe I didn't have a purpose. Maybe I'd made a mistake and took a wrong turn somewhere and missed my calling altogether. If you've ever felt this way, give me a high five and hang tight because I'm here to bring you some hope!

Not until I was 43 years old and about six months into my network marketing business did I have the revelation of all revelations. Every stinkin' odd job I'd ever held—and let me tell you, there were *dozens*—had led to this experience. I could suddenly look back on my life and see how every seemingly dead-end job had taught me some skill that I was now using to build my business. I had clarity that the jobs didn't last because I had learned what I needed to learn from them, and it was time to move on and learn the next skill. It was almost like I had been in school, going from class to class, learning what I needed that would then help me get to the next level in my life. If you're struggling right now, you're probably thinking, "Oh, well, good for you, Shari Brown. Must be nice." Well, yes, it is nice, *but* that's not my point.

My point is that there's nothing special about me, so if this is happening for me, it's happening for you too! It happens for all of us. I've coached countless women, shared this story with them, and watched as they began connecting the dots of their own past. There's something very freeing about the clarity you get when you can see that there's been guidance and a pattern in your life. For some it's more obvious than for others, but I guarantee you that there's a pattern for you too. The more you look for it and pay attention, the more you'll notice it!

You have unique skills and perspectives that you've developed based on the life you've lived. *You* have an important voice in this world because there's nobody out there quite like you. Even if you think it's been done before, or if you think it's been done better, if you have the desire to do it, then you need to *do* it! Because nobody will do it quite like you.

I've had to give myself this pep talk many, many times—even while writing this book! Is the content new? No. Has it been written about and said a million times? I'm pretty sure it has. But this is the first time *I'm* bringing *my* voice, my experience, my stories, and my perspective to the table. This book is a part of *my* journey, and I'm the only one who gets a say in what I do with my energy and my life!

Try this exercise: Grab a pen and paper, and complete the following sentences to really see the magic. Look back on your life, go as far back as you'd like, and play this game:

Because I had this [name a job/experience] _____, it led me to this [name the place/situation/experience] _____. And because I was led to that [place/situation/experience] _____, I [met someone/learned something] _____, which then led me to [a lesson or a gift that I gained from the experience] _____.

Here's my example, "Because I was pregnant, it led me to an online mom group. And because I was led to that online mom group, I met Tami, which then led to me joining her network marketing business."

You could play that game forever! But truly, look how miraculous it is when you see it on paper. Look at how the most seemingly random things happened that caused you to do or decide something or meet someone, and that then led you to different places and experiences. I like to think I have so much control over my life, but when I look at this exercise, I realize that I've really been guided. Sometimes it's almost scary to think how easily I could have missed some of the greatest things in my life if it hadn't been for a few small random choices. This exercise really helps ground me when I have moments where I feel unsure of the future, or when I'm worried about something. I think back on stuff that worried me when I was in high school and college, and I remind myself that it all worked itself out. Things that devastated me in my twenties and thirties, I wouldn't change at all because of what came as a result of those experiences. I'm sure you've been through some tough stuff in your life too, and while you wouldn't want to go through it again, positives can come from every situation.

When I remind myself of that, the current situation doesn't seem so scary. If you can look forward with the same confidence and trust that you have when looking back at the challenges you've overcome in your life, you can manage your fear and remain in action. Ultimately, if it won't matter in six months or one year, then it doesn't matter.

Being an entrepreneur is 90% mindset. Because without an open, coachable mindset, you won't ever hit your full potential. The smallest things will take you down. You won't stand a chance against the big stuff. But those who know that everything is always working out for them, that every problem has a solution, and that "this too shall pass"—those people stick around and learn new ways to work and pivot. Those are the people who become great leaders and build large businesses. They leave a legacy of inspiration and help countless numbers of people who are looking for a better quality of life.

Have you ever heard the story about the twin brothers whose father committed a crime when they were little and spent his life in prison? When the boys were grown, one brother ended up on death row, and the other became a successful business-man. When they were asked, "Why do you think your life ended up the way that it did?" they both gave the same answer: "It's because of my father. What other choice did I have?" This is the *perfect* example of how mindset is everything. Also, it shows that you have the power to decide what something means. The story that you tell yourself will either *give* you power or take power away from you. What will you choose? #thisshouldbe-obvious #icangiveyoutheanswer #itsthefirstone

PART TWO

Making Money

The Modern-Day Handbook for Selling Success

6

Cannonball!

*Opportunity is missed by
most people because it is dressed
in overalls and looks like work.*
THOMAS EDISON

Jump into the Deep End of the Pool!

Now that you've established the proper mindset, let's set you up to win! While there's no guarantee for success, one thing is a guarantee for failure: dipping your toe in the water. If you want a shot at success, you've got to *cannonball* into the deep end of the pool!

When I began my network marketing business, I had a serious talk with myself. I had been in sales and knew enough from running my own business as a massage therapist that if I was really going to do this ... I needed to *do this*. I had to be all in, full blast, pedal to the metal. I had learned over the years that if you're timid when you begin because you are afraid of looking foolish, or if you're worried about what others might think, or you just want to "see how it goes" before committing fully, you will fail. Guaranteed! That's partly why I hadn't joined before— because I knew that I had to be in a place where I was ready to go full steam ahead or I would be wasting my time and energy. You will never know what you are capable of if you don't give it all you've got. Even if I fail, peeps gotta respect my hustle! And I know that I'm going to learn something along the way, even if I lose—because there really is no losing. It's all winning or learning. And heaven knows it's going to make a great Rocking Chair Story either way!

Over the years I've seen and coached tens of thousands of women, and what I know for sure is that we are all very similar.

Yes, I was nervous! *Yes*, I worried about what my tiny number of Facebook followers were going to think and say about me. But I needed to do this for my family. If you're a mama, you know we will do things for our kids that we wouldn't do for another soul on this Earth, including ourselves. I decided that since I was the one paying my bills and responsible for the well-being of my children, I wasn't going to hand over my life decisions to other people's opinions. #canigetanamen As I've gotten older, I feel like this is really the big lesson we are all here to learn. Live your life. That's it. Live *your* life. Allow others to live *their* lives. You do you. They do them. So simple, but not so easy, right?

It was time to take a deep breath and cannonball into that deep end of the pool! I decided that my first Facebook post was going to be calling out the elephant in the room. Maybe it was the years of being teased mercilessly as a kid that taught me that it's better to "out yourself" and say what you know others are going to say. It went something like this: "Hey friends! Okay, so guess what I'm doing? Prepare yourselves mentally and emotionally, and get ready to roll your eyes, but I have fallen *so hard in love* with this product that I don't ever want to be without it. So I am now selling it! Here's why I love it so much..."

I posted daily about my joy, my gratitude, and what the product and the business were doing for me, my family, and the women on my team. I didn't post ads; I posted about me and my life. I learned that enthusiasm buys you grace from your followers. What I mean by that is that if you see someone posting about something and they are super excited and happy, it's less annoying. Your audience will smile and laugh and maybe shake their heads, but they've gotta give you props for your energy and enthusiasm! Even if they get tired of hearing you talk about it, they will admire your hustle.

Get out of
your own way.

It's Not Them—It's You

Fear is a wicked beast! It can make us do things, and it can especially make us *not* do things. Whenever I'm coaching someone who is throwing every excuse in the book at me about why she can't build a business or why it won't work, I know I'm talking to the fear monster. The worst response is, "I've already done that, and it doesn't work. I can't make money here." Listen, in the words of Tom "Big Al" Schreiter, in his book *How to Build Network Marketing Leaders*, "If there is someone in your organization making money, it can be done." And *no*, you don't have to get into the company in the early years. Timing means nothing if you don't work your business! All those excuses come from fear, and it makes people uncoachable. If you want to grow, you need to be open. You need a coachable mindset. A coachable mindset says, "Okay, I've tried that technique before and didn't have much success. Maybe there's a piece I was missing. Can you show me what you're talking about?" Now this is someone I can help! Together we can come up with a plan. #aaahhhfeelssogood

An "uncoachable" mindset says, "Been there. Done that. Doesn't work. Did that too. And that doesn't work either. This business doesn't work." Ummm... every business *can* work if you're open to learning and bettering your skills. But there's no room in an uncoachable mindset for problem solving or brainstorming. As a coach, that means I'm hitting a brick wall. Can you feel how the energy of the coachable mindset is different? Hopeful? Eager? The uncoachable mindset is shut off, resistant, and fighting for limitations.

One woman on my team, Brandy, was struggling and couldn't figure out how to lift her business off the ground. I recognized immediately that Brandy was really worried about what she *thought* other people were saying about her and her online business. Nobody had said anything to her directly, but she was so consumed with what they *might* say that it stifled her. Her posts weren't fully her, and they lacked enthusiasm. She was dipping a toe in the shallow end of the pool, and what she needed was the ginormous splash from doing a cannonball into the deep end of the pool to kick that business off with a bang! #Geronimo

I explained to Brandy what I've discovered about enthusiasm. I've observed over the last 30-plus years in sales that enthusiasm transfers by half. Here's what I mean—imagine I am *super* excited about something and I'm bouncing out of my chair. Let's say I'm at a level 10 on the enthusiasm scale. I share this *super-duper* excitement with you, and you get excited too! In my experience, the *most* excited another person will be is about half of where you are. So, if I am a 10 (full-blown *cannonball* level), the most you could be is a 5. If I'm a 5 (cautiously dipping a toe in the shallow end), the most you could be is a 2.5... meh. Now, of course this isn't an exact science, just an observation, but quite often I've seen this to be the case. To give yourself the absolute best shot at success, you've got to be *in it* and *pumped*!

Brandy and I made a list of the people in her life who loved her and only wanted the best for her. She wrote their names down and put them up on the wall so she could see them when she went live on social media. I told her to imagine that she was just hanging out with only those people, and to be her absolute authentic self. Be a goofball if that's who she really was! Be quirky, funny, sarcastic, whatever! Brandy felt like she needed some support, so she reached out to a few of her friends and invited them to join her when she went live. She showed up with tons of energy and smiles, and that energy pumped life back into her business! She was *fun* to watch! It took some practice, but it wasn't long before she was showing up solely focused on her raving fans and not giving any mental energy to her critics. And by the way, she never confirmed that anyone was criticizing her in the first place. It was just a story she was telling herself. And even if it was true, *who cares*?! The peanut gallery isn't paying the bills! #youdoyouboo

Gretchen Rubin says in her book *The Happiness Project*, "Act the way you want to feel." It's true. When you show up with enthusiasm, even if you've got to fake it till you make it in the very beginning, you will create a wave of energy that comes back to you. You'll notice more engagement in your posts and live streams, which will energize *you*, and so the cycle goes.

I'm not a huge fan of "fake it till you make it," but I will tell you that when I worked retail, there were so many days that I was just not feeling it. Maybe I was tired or stressed from school; maybe I'd had an argument with my boyfriend—whatever it was. But I had to work and pay the bills. I worked on commission, so if I didn't fully show up, someone else would get the sale and make the money. Even on bad days, I put that smile on my face and faked it for the first ten minutes or so of my shift. I say ten minutes because here's what I discovered: When I smiled and pretended to be enthusiastic and happy, it wasn't too long before I felt better! I felt happier, lighter, and more energetic. I didn't forget my problems, but I wasn't living in that energy.

Same goes for your online business. It is a *business*. It is a *job*. You don't get to decide whether to show up to a nine-to-five job—not if you want to stay employed! Same goes for your network marketing job. Like I tell my 12-year-old when he doesn't want to brush his teeth: "You only have to brush the teeth you want to keep." You don't have to show up for your business... unless you want to keep your business. Show up with a smile, in the spirit of servant leadership, providing value for your customers and team, and the feelings will follow!

This is probably a good time to tell you that if you think network marketing is easy money, you're wrong. #butSharievery-onealwayssaysthat #IsaidwhatIsaid Look, it's definitely *easier* money than many jobs, in my opinion, because of the time freedom and flexibility. But it's still a job! For over eight years, I've shown up every single day because in my mind, absence is not an option. Ooh, that should be a hashtag! #absenceisnot-anoption Now, some days I've worked 15-plus hours, some days I'm in it for just two hours, and sometimes I'm on vacation. But just like a nine-to-five job, I come back from my vacation and get back to work. I don't expect the business to work if I don't. I don't expect my team to work if I don't. I come from a place of service, and I ask, "Who can I help today?"

If Your Mouth Is Closed, So Is Your Business

We can talk and talk about business and selling strategies, or the latest social media tricks, but none of those things will help if you don't get the basics down. When I say basics, I mean *talk about what you are doing*. Is your business your best-kept secret? As Steuart (yes, that is how his mama spelled it) Henderson Britt said in his book *Marketing Management and Administrative Action*, "Doing business without advertising is like winking at a girl in the dark. You know what you are doing but nobody else does." So are you talking about your business with enthusiasm and pride? You are an entrepreneur; you are self-employed! Be proud of it! When I'm coaching, I always make the comparison of an online business and a brick-and-mortar store. Let's say you open a pizza business. Are you just going to open the doors one day and not tell anyone about it? Just for fun, let's take four very common sentiments that I hear daily and apply them to our pizza business example:

- I'm not sure if I feel like opening the restaurant today.

- I don't want people to think that I just want their money.

- I don't want to bother people by talking about my pizza business.

- I feel bad selling pizza and trying to earn a living.

Do you hear how absolutely ridiculous this sounds and see how that business is 100% going to fail? So why would your online business be any different?

I can't tell you how many times people have come to me so upset and distraught that the "business doesn't work," and when I look at their social media, I see nothing. By "nothing," I mean that if we aren't friends on social media, I see absolutely nothing there but a profile picture because their privacy settings are locked down tight. No mention that they even *have* a business! If we *are* friends on social media, I can see their posts, but I have to scroll and scroll to find one post or one mention about their business. They don't mention where they work in their bio, and there's no link to their website. You don't have to be Nancy Drew to figure out why they're not selling anything!

If you own that pizza shop and only unlock the door or show up one day a month, how much pizza do you think you can sell? Stop expecting your online business to work when you don't. The business works! *Any* business works if you do what it takes to make it work.

> **HOT TIP!** Building a business takes commitment and work, whether it's online or not. You need to show up consistently. *No. Matter. What.*

Be the Connector

. . . .

Do you know those people who always "have a guy"? My husband is like that. Need new tires on your car? He's got a guy. Have a plumbing issue? He's got a guy. Actually, he will always say, "You should go see *my buddy* down at the tire shop." It's a running joke now because I'll ask if he has a *buddy* when I need something. I call these people "connectors," and if you aren't like that, I'm sure you know someone who is! This is your go-to person when you need something because they always have a connection somewhere. These people are a gift! It's such a great feeling to have someone whom you trust give you a recommendation, isn't it? Do you see where I'm headed with this? #winkwink #nudgenudge

You can be a connector! How wonderful would it be for your friends and followers to have a person they could go to with questions and advice for whatever issue your product can solve? Whatever company you're with, you're there because you love the products. Think about why you love them, and share that with as many people as you can. "I had this problem, and now I don't," or, "I was dealing with xyz, and here's how I took care of it." Think about the person who introduced *you* to the products you're selling. Aren't you so happy that they shared them with you? There are so many people out there who could benefit from your products or from the extra income they received from selling.

When Melinda and I started working together, she was frustrated that her business wasn't growing. She thought that maybe the momentum and hype of the business had passed, and she had missed the boat. I knew other people who were killin' it in their business, so I knew it wasn't a case of missing the boat. It only took two seconds to figure out the problem once I looked at her social media accounts. Her settings were locked

"Doing business without advertising is like winking at a girl in the dark.
You know what you are doing but nobody else does."

STEUART HENDERSON BRITT

down *tight*. I couldn't see a thing! When I mentioned that to her, she said that she didn't feel comfortable making her posts public because she wanted to protect her family. Who *doesn't* want to protect their family? I get that, but there's a way to talk publicly about your business without putting your family at risk.

I explained that if she wasn't willing to talk about her business, then just like the pizza example, she would be out of business. To grow a business online, you can't be public with business but keep your personal life private. It simply won't work. As Simon Sinek says in his book *Find Your Why*, "People don't buy *what* you do; they buy *why* you do it." People will buy from people they trust, and if you're just posting about your business and not sharing who you are and why your business is important to you, you're just another ad. There's nothing personal there to connect people to you.

There are so many ways to talk about your life without exposing everything. For example, you can post pictures of your kids without showing their faces. Maybe they are running down the street away from you and you're taking a selfie with them in the background, or maybe you're taking them out for ice cream, and you post a picture of the ice cream without anyone's face in the shot. If you want to post a picture so that Grandma and Aunt Shirley can see it, then just change the privacy settings for that particular post and select the audience you want. However you decide to do it, share your life to show other people that you're just like them. Build rapport and trust, and let them know that if they have a question or need something, you're their go-to person. #heybuddy

By creating a new plan, Melinda made a few thoughtful tweaks to her posts and made them public. By being consistent, she began to see changes in her business! She was gaining more followers and interaction on her posts. More importantly, she was focused on helping people and being their connector by solving problems with her products. It breathed life back into her! She was surprised to see how many of her friends commented and congratulated her on her "new" business. Ummm... she had been in business for over two years. #yikes (Seriously, I need emojis!)

HOT TIP! Want to create quick momentum in your business? It's a very simple formula: Take lots of action in a short period of time. That's it! Think about it; are you going to create more momentum by following up with ten customers in a month or ten customers in a week or even a day? Are you going to create more momentum going live on social media once a week or daily for a week? Challenge yourself and make a game out of it! Invite others in your business to do it with you, and hold each other accountable. You don't need a 30-day plan. You can create a seven-day, a five-day, or even a three-day plan and then repeat it.

Bodies in motion tend to stay in motion, so find what works for you and gets you into action. You will feel so good, I promise! Sitting and thinking about what you're *not* doing is ten times more stressful and exhausting that just doing the dang thing. #onyourmarkgetset

7

Houston, You Have a Networking Problem

To be interesting, be interested.
DALE CARNEGIE

Friends and Family Aren't the Destination—They're the Doorway!

"But Shari, my friends and family don't buy from me." Okay, let's get this one out of the way right now, once and for all. Don't expect your friends and family to buy! Let it go, and let's move on, k? K. Besides, you will never build a strong business on the backs of friends and family, so don't worry if they aren't buying. There are countless reasons why they don't buy from you, especially when you are just starting out in your business. Here are just a few:

1 They may be waiting to see if you *really* like the product before they buy it. If you've bounced from company to company, you may have lost some of their trust.

2 They might be afraid that if they buy and then don't like the product, it will be awkward.

3 They might worry that you're going to hound them to keep buying more, and they don't want to have to say no to you.

4 They already have a product that they love, and they don't want to switch.

Remember, it's not their responsibility to buy from you or to support your new venture. That statement might shock you, but it's true. If your sales are low, you don't have a sales problem; you simply don't know enough people—yet! And feeling like nobody will buy from you is a typical self-limiting belief. We're going to fix that! Let's learn how to find new people and make connections.

Cathleen came to me a few months into her business. She said she couldn't get her business off the ground because her friends didn't have money. I gave her the same advice—don't try to build your business on the backs of friends and family. It wouldn't work past the first week, even if your friends had a ton of money! In fact, you should be through this "warm market" (people whom you already know) within your first two weeks.

But, as I told Cathleen, every one of your friends, even those you've known all your life, have friends and acquaintances whom you don't know yet. Don't think so? Go to their Facebook profile page and see how many mutual friends you have compared with your total number of friends. At some point, you either went to different schools, had different jobs, or married into different families—and the list goes on!

Cathleen also assumed that her friends couldn't afford the products. Listen, I struggled financially most of my life, but for some reason, every time I walked into Target it was $80 out of my pocket. It's not your job to make financial decisions for someone else. We are going to dive deeper into these concepts in chapter 8, but for now, just know that your best approach is to let people know what's on the menu and stay out of their wallets. #theirmoneyistheirbusiness

When Cathleen began to shift her mindset and see her friends and family as the doorway to a bigger clientele, rather than as her final destination, we could focus on finding people outside her warm market. I love this part because it's where you get to play and spread kindness! Here's how you do it:

1   Search for a Facebook group that's devoted to the hobbies and things you enjoy. Yoga, wine, cooking, reading, exercise (I mean, okay... if that's your thing), dogs, cats, shopping, shoes, things you collect, favorite TV shows—the options are endless!

2   Join the group. But here's the golden rule: Do not ever, ever, *ever* discuss your business in these groups! You are there to become a genuine part of the community.

3   Every day, before you post about your business on your Facebook profile, spend at least 15 minutes in these groups. You don't have to post in the group; just respond to other people's posts by "loving" the post and commenting, with *four words or more.* If possible, ask a question in your comment. If you get a response from the author of the post, even better! Doing this will tell the Facebook algorithm that you are interested in this person, and besides that, you are building a relationship with them.

4   Now, go post something on your Facebook profile. Since you've spent some time engaging with others, this post will potentially gain more views.

5   As you're meeting people and building relationships, consider going to their Facebook or Instagram profiles and commenting on *their* stories. The beauty of stories is that any comment you make goes directly to their inbox as an actual message! Remember, *do not* ever mention your business. Be a person. Build that friendship! If you follow these steps, people will see what you do for a living, and they will appreciate that you didn't try to sell to them. Also, you don't look like you're desperate for sales, even if you are! #becool #patience-younggrasshopper I've found that people are more likely to buy from me when I don't mention my business directly to them. They see my posts, so they know!

I have met some of my very best friends in online groups, so don't underestimate their value. In fact, I wouldn't have found this business, changed my family's life forever, or even be writing this book if it hadn't been for the friendships I made in an online group. #thanksTami

Building a business is all about growing a large community or network. The more people you know, the more referrals you can get, and the bigger you can grow. If you want to personally sell thousands of dollars a month, are you more likely to do that with a network of 20 people or with a network of 200 people? Running your own business isn't just a wish; it's math. If your average customer spends $50 on your products every three months, how many customers do you need to be able to sell $500 per month, month after month? (Hint: You need 30 regular customers. #salesmathistheonlymathIcando) We will get into the details about how to make that happen, but first let's build the groundwork!

And Then She Told Five Friends...

Yes, posting on your social media is critical, but you also need to be building relationships and having conversations with people. So I want you to think of five people in your life with whom you're close enough to that you can say the following:

> Hey! I need your help. I'm trying to build a network for my new business, and I'm doing a free online event. It's going to be lots of fun, and I'm showing people how to *[name a problem that your hero product solves]*. Don't worry; I don't expect you to buy anything, but can you invite 25 or more of your friends to the event? I'll give you the message to send to them, and I'll also reach out to introduce myself so they don't feel like they've been spammed.

How you view and treat
your customers will
**determine the strength
of your business.**

I did this with some of the moms from my kids' school, and in exchange, one friend made me promise to volunteer at the school carnival—which felt like selling my soul to the devil. (I kid! I kid!) #kinda But it was a small price to pay to increase my contact list and broaden my network!

Think about it. If you have five friends who each introduce you to 25 people, that's 125 new contacts. If you can find five people from those 125 people and repeat the event, that's another 125 new people! Now, not all of them will buy from you right away. *Let. That. Go.* Some people will watch you for a year or more before buying. It's all about planting seeds. Sales aren't the determining factor to a successful event. Just meeting one new person is a win! Remember, they are the *doorway*!

Now, what do these events look like? This is where you can be as creative as you want to be. You can create an event or a group on Facebook and go live to teach something. Remember that you must give value before you expect anything in return. First, do your homework and make a list of the problems that your products can solve. If that feels overwhelming, just focus on your favorite product!

I often hear that people are worried that they're annoying their followers by talking about their business so much. But in the next breath, they say that nobody is seeing their posts. Well, which is it? Can't be both. #realitycheck This is fear talking, and once again, these are stories you're telling yourself! If you have enthusiasm and are bringing value to the table, then other people's opinions belong to them, not you. Make a business plan and stick to it! Create a calendar and plan your content. It doesn't have to be complicated. Simple is best. What is your theme for Monday? Tuesday? And so on.

Focus on Your Hero Product

I'd like to tell you that when I built my business, I had a grand business plan and a vision. Ha! #nopeonarope All I knew was that I loved our hero product, the mascara! Every company has a hero product, by the way. It's that one product that either nobody else has or that your company does better than anyone else. Now, let's say you're with a company that has many hero products. Yay! That's fantastic—but if you're nervous about starting your business, please follow my advice and just focus on one product. Not only will it be simpler, but it's also more effective.

Social media is a crowded place, and it's becoming harder and harder to get views and be seen. Back in the early 1930s, they used to say that it took a consumer seeing the same or similar images seven times before they would buy. Now that social media is on the scene, that number is said to be closer to 77. #whoa

Because of the overcrowding on social, it's imperative that you start off with a clear and concise message. What do you want your followers to know about your hero product? Can it be conveyed in three sentences or fewer? The shorter the better! Can it be shown in a simple photo? Humor works really well too! Is there a way to say something funny in your post? #friendsdontletfriendshavelittlelashes #likethat

Being clear on your message and then finding a few different ways to get that message across with selfies, short videos, or lives will help you cut through the clutter. Some people prefer videos and going live, but you also want to be able to capture the customer who might not be in a place where they can watch a video. They could be standing in line at Target, in a meeting or class, surrounded by screaming preschoolers, or pretending to listen to their spouse tell a story—you just never know! #totallyhypothetical So sprinkle in some selfie posts with your videos!

In his book *Jab, Jab, Jab, Right Hook*, Gary Vaynerchuk lays out some excellent social media strategies. First, you've got to hit your audience with a series of jabs and then a solid right hook for that knockout punch! The jabs can be posts about your life; sharing something inspiring; or asking for advice on a movie, a recipe, or an appliance purchase, for example. The right hook is a post about your business. Those initial jabs are *so important*! You don't want to be all about the business because... well, *ewww*. Not only is that ineffective, but it's boring. Now, let's say that you drop a "right hook" today with a picture of you using your product. Tomorrow your right hook is to go live and talk about it, and the next day you can post a short video. (Don't forget that you need a few "jabs" about your life and interests in between!) I love to take videos with my phone and then use a video editing app (such as VivaVideo or VideoShow) to speed that video up to twice the speed and add some music.

> **HOT TIP!** When you create your videos or pictures, make sure they are "evergreen." That means that there's no reference to the date or season. You can use evergreen content again and again, and it still feels fresh. No Christmas trees in the background or references to it being summertime. This is such a time saver, and before you know it, you'll find yourself with a library of content that you can use over and over. Make sure to save these videos in an album on your phone for easy access, and don't forget to upload them to YouTube! It's the second-largest search engine, and since you've already done the work, put it to good use!

Let me give you an example of why focusing on one hero product is so important and effective when starting out. Let's say you have ten products that you love, and you post about one product each day. In ten days your customer has seen each product only once. In a month they've seen each product only three times. That's in addition to the thousands of other products and ads they see daily. Your message and products are diluted, so they won't make the same impact as if you are posting about the same product with different variations of posts—like pictures, videos, and lives—five times per week. By the end of the month, your customers will have seen your product 20 times. They know what you sell because you've just penetrated the noise on social media! They get it! If the message is concise, they could probably tell *you* all about it.

Now, does this mean you never mention the other products? *No!* You can still talk about them, but those posts are *extra*! They are in addition to your original plan. Whether you're brand new, are wanting to get back in the game, or just feel overwhelmed, focus on getting that hero product into the hands of as many people as you can, as quickly as you can. You really can start a business with just one amazing product!

When someone buys your hero product, you should follow up with them several times:

- Thank them for their order.

- Let them know when it will be shipped.

- Check in a few days after they receive it to see how they like it, and answer questions.

Once they've tried the product and love it, you can mention the other products that might enhance that product. I am personally a fan of what they call a "soft sell." I don't like to be aggressive because I don't like salespeople who are aggressive with me. After I've completed all of the above follow-up, I like to say something like this: "I'm so happy you love it! Listen, next time you're ready to order, check out this product: [name the product]. I love to use it with [the item they bought] because [tell them what problem it solved for you or how it enhanced your life]." For example, "Net time you're ready to order, check out the cleansing balm! I love to use it to remove my mascara and makeup because it works quickly and makes my skin so soft!"

"It takes months to find a customer, seconds to lose one."

VINCE LOMBARDI

This is the best way I know to give great customer service, let them know what you have to offer, and then give them space. People appreciate the information but don't feel pressured. In my experience, when people feel pressured, they won't come back. Or maybe that's just me? Lol. #backoff

> **HOT TIP!** Asking for referrals at the end of every conversation is another great way to build your network. It's as simple as saying, "If you have any friends who you think would be interested, feel free to give them my info!" You are much more likely to buy a product based on a recommendation from someone you know and trust. Relationships and referrals are the best way to slice right through all the ads that bombard us on a daily basis!

The ABC's of Networking

If you've been in business for more than a couple of months, you know that feeling every month when you see your numbers start out at $0. Ugh! Every month we begin again! It's a fresh start, and if you don't carry the end-of-month momentum over into the new month, it can feel like starting from scratch and pushing a car up a hill. I get it!

First things first—it's time for a mindset check! All businesses start fresh on the first day of the month; it's just how it's done. Companies track numbers monthly, quarterly, and yearly. So you're not the only one. Now, let's focus on what we can do to get those numbers up as quickly as possible! Quite often I see teams that have a big sales month, then a slow month or two, then another big month.

I know a lot of people think that if they had huge sales months one after the other, it would be amazing! This might surprise you, but I'm here to tell you that that's not always the best way to grow. Not only will you burn out, but you will very likely lose a huge opportunity! The reality is that when you have a really busy month, follow-up falls to the wayside. When you don't follow up, it's like throwing a beautiful gift in the trash. You made the sale, your work paid off, and someone trusted you enough to purchase—so take care of that person! I always felt like I made the most strides in growing my business in the slower months because I had the time to connect with my customers. The goal isn't to just make one sale; the goal is to build a relationship so that you have many sales over the years, and you continue to provide value to that person. She will then tell her friends about you and the product, and because of that referral, you don't have to work so hard to gain their trust. Those conversations can lead to bigger sales in the months where you do the follow-up, and then your sales will grow even more in the busy months!

We've discussed how it's easier to hit big numbers if you have 200 customers vs. 20 customers. #totesobvi Your goal is always to continue networking and building your community and relationships with people. Time for some more math. If your average sale is $50, and you have 20 customers, then the most you can sell in a month is $1,000. If you have 200 customers and your average sale is $50, you could sell $10,000 in a month! (Can I get a *wahoo* for that commission check?!) Now, that $10,000 can only happen if *every single one* of your 200 customers makes a purchase in the same month. That rarely happens, but in a big month like November, when people are in the shopping spirit, it can happen. It's a wonderful, glorious unicorn of a month, and one that we are all so grateful for— but remember that it is *not* the norm! In fact, when I'm coaching and looking at someone's sales numbers, I glance at November, but I don't put much focus on it. Even a squirrel gets a nut now and then, and November is good for just about everybody, so it doesn't tell the whole story.

I like to study people's behavior, and I realized early on in my career that the average customer for beauty products would buy something every three months on average. Depending on the usage rate of the products you're selling, your customers might buy less or possibly more often, but for this example, let's use a typical reorder of every three months. The more connection I have with a customer, the more conversations we are likely to have, and the more I can recommend items that would benefit her. So as the relationship grows, the average sale grows. But even then, she's not always interested in buying something monthly. So now what do you do?

Customer Purchasing Patterns

Group A Most likely to make repeat purchases in	Group B Most likely to make repeat purchases in	Group C Most likely to make repeat purchases in
JANUARY A	FEBRUARY B	MARCH C
APRIL A	MAY B	JUNE C
JULY A	AUGUST B	SEPTEMBER C
OCTOBER A	NOVEMBER B	DECEMBER C

This is where the ABC's of networking come in! To start building up more consistent sales month to month, consider developing three "groups" of customers. It goes something like this: Group A made a purchase in January. A few customers in

Group A might buy something again in February or March, but typically Group A will be *most likely* to purchase again in April. Group B are the people who purchased in February. Group B will be most likely to purchase again in May. Group C bought from you in March, so they would typically need a refill in June. If you're a visual person like me, the graphic will help explain it a bit better!

Grouping your customers will help you evaluate where there's opportunity to grow. Do you have plenty of customers in Group A, but your B months are typically slower? I keep track of them either in a notebook or on index cards in a recipe box. If you're fancy like Applebees, you can create a spreadsheet. I don't know how to do that sort of sorcery, so don't ask me! #oldschool

So if Group A is big and bought a lot in April, you can get an idea that those people will need to refill their product and potentially buy again in July, *if* you follow up. If your July was slow but your April was big, what is that telling you? Hint: Fortune is in the follow-up! It's possible you weren't checking in on them and building rapport. And to be honest, if that's the case, then you dropped the ball and let your customer down. She bought a product from you, and she deserves your time and attention, so don't be afraid to reach out!

> **HOT TIP!** Message your customer *today* if you realized you dropped the ball!
>
> "Hey, Stacy! How are you? I'm so sorry I haven't checked in on you; business has been crazy busy! How is it going with your [insert product here]?"

Taking a good hard look at the number of customers you have and the months in which they purchased will show you that you probably haven't been having big sales months consistently because you simply don't have enough of a customer base, or your follow-up is lackin' in the crackin'. Instead of just tracking sales, how about you dig deeper and look at the number of customers and their average sale? Increase the number of customers and their average sale, and you will increase your overall sales! Build those customers, and you'll have more people purchasing from you month after month. Again, it's not magic—it's math.

Do You Have Clients or Customers?

What comes to mind when you hear someone say they have customers vs. having clients? To me a customer is an acquaintance. It's someone whom you may or may not have a relationship with. A client, on the other hand, feels completely different. This is someone who does regular business with you, and there is a relationship and trust between the two of you. I've found that when I think of my customers as *clients,* it changes my expectations for myself and how I need to treat them. It reminds me that I am a person they trust, and it's my job to make sure they get the best customer service that I can provide. It's important to think long-term. Your client is someone who means more than just one or two sales. This is a relationship that you want to last for years. Once you've established that relationship, it's so much easier to suggest products that you think she'd benefit from. So you're essentially talking to a friend, sending messages such as this:

> Hi Mary, our new [insert product] launches tomorrow, and it works perfectly with the [insert product] that you're already using. Here's the link to check it out! [insert link]
>
> By the way, how was your vacay? It looked amazing! I was living vicariously through you!

Note: Did you notice how I got right down to business in that message and *then* followed up with a personal comment? It's important to get right to the reason for your message up front! More on this in a minute.

Customers come and go, but a client has loyalty and is there to stay. The best part is that it's *so much fun* to work with people whom you've built a relationship with!

Fortune Is in the Follow-up

The biggest missing link in any business is lack of follow-up. People seem to be afraid to reach out, but I'm here to tell you that you need to be afraid *not* to reach out. Here are my "Five Steps to Follow-up." This is a general guideline because every relationship is different, so use your best judgment, and remember to follow your intuition with each customer.

So you got a sale—*yay!* This one sale is the doorway to a *relationship*. You don't just want a one-and-done sale; you want a *client*. So let's go!

Step 1: The Thank-You (within 24 to 36 hours)

Once you receive notice of the purchase from the company website, thank your client (let's call her Stacy) for the sale. Let her know you'll be tracking her purchase and letting her know when it ships.

Step 2: The Shipping Notification

Let her know when the product ships. Send an email, DM, or text to say, "Hey, Stacy, your order is on its way!" #easypeasy

Step 3: The Two-Week Follow-up

Two weeks after she's ordered, send a message: "Hey, Stacy! By now you should have received your items; how do you like them?"

Enthusiasm sells, but it transfers by half.

Do not be afraid to ask this question! Listen, you want the good, the bad, and the ugly. *Do not* be afraid that they won't like something. You will make it right no matter what! My *best* and most loyal customers were those who had an issue with an item, whether it was user error or the product simply wasn't for them. This gave me the *opportunity* to show my customer service skills, and it gave us a chance to have more conversations and get to know each other better! When you know that you're going to make that customer happy no matter what, you can relax. The last thing you want is for her to keep quiet about a product that she isn't happy with—because if she doesn't tell you, she won't buy from you again, and you'll have no chance to redeem yourself. You are now about to earn her trust by showing her that you're on her side. That is priceless, and she will most definitely tell her friends how amazing you are!

Step 4: The Four-Week Follow-up

Check back four weeks after she ordered: "Hi, Stacy! Just checking in to see how it's going with your [insert product name]." I always encourage my customer to give me her honest opinion: "I really want your honest opinion, so don't hold back!" This enables you to troubleshoot if there are any issues. For example, if she's not getting the best results, you can recommend solutions. Also, this shows Stacy that you aren't afraid to hear bad news! It shows her that you are confident in your product and in your ability to make it right.

Step 5: The Eight-Week Refill Reminder

Eight weeks after the sale, write to say, "Hey, Stacy, how is it going?" Wait to see if she responds so the exchange is more conversational. If she doesn't respond within a couple of days, you can write, "You should be getting low on your [insert product name here]. When you're ready for a refill, here's your link.

If you aren't already using the [insert a product that goes with the product she's already purchased from you], check it out! It works great with your [name of product she has already purchased] because [give her the benefits]. As always, I'm here if you have questions! Have a great day!" For example, if she bought mascara, you could suggest that she try the lash primer because it will help to condition her lashes.

After that eight-week mark, make sure Stacy is in your calendar so that you are intentionally commenting on her social media posts and stories every other week or so. Comment with a minimum of four words. That shows the "powers that be" that you are friends and helps your algorithm. And when you have products that you think Stacy would like, don't be afraid to let her know. It can be as simple as this: "Hey, Stacy! I know you love [product name], and this [related product] works great with it! My customers typically use these together and love it because it [list the benefits]. I hope you're well! I loved your [comment on a recent post of hers]!"

And *always* let your customers know when there's a sale!

Be Clear and Direct

When I'm messaging a customer, I always keep in mind something that I learned in a YouTube video from Simon Sinek, author of *Find Your Why*. He'd received a message from an old friend from college. They hadn't spoken in years. The message began with, "Hey, Simon. How are you? Let's get together for coffee." Simon thought this was odd because it was so out of the blue. And then he read on: "Oh, by the way, I am starting a new business and wanted to run it by you." *Aaahhh*, there it was. Sinek rolled his eyes and never responded.

He gave some great advice about messaging someone: Start the conversation with your reason for messaging. If the old college friend above had written, "Hey, Simon, it's been a long time! I have this business opportunity that I wanted to run by you," and *then* added in, "I hope you're doing well; let's get together for coffee and catch up," the entire dynamic would have changed. The request to get together sounds more genuine when it follows your "ask." As Sinek wisely pointed out, when you receive a message from someone out of the blue, you're always thinking, "What do they want?" Get that out of the way first so that the pleasantries feel more genuine! #genius

If you've never intentionally built a network before, all the tips in this chapter may feel like a lot. I *promise* you that if you take it one step at a time, it won't take long before you have developed habits that will become second nature! It's the repetition and consistency of simple steps that will grow and multiply. Before you know it, you are going to have an incredible community of loyal customers who are so grateful for the service you provide!

8

The Art of Non-selling

*Courteous treatment will make
a customer a walking advertisement.*
UNKNOWN

Be the Waiter!

I take issue with Elton John. I don't think "sorry" is the hardest word. I think the hardest word is "no"! So many of us live in fear of the word "no," myself included. Is it that we are afraid of rejection? Are our egos that fragile? Probably. Maybe our self-worth is so tied up in what others think about us that to ask a question where we just might hear the word "no" would crush our souls. I mean, how many "no"s can one human handle? I don't think any of us would volunteer to find out!

So how do we come to terms with the *big fear* of "no" and still sell effectively in a way that feels good to both the seller and the client? That's where the "art of non-selling" comes into play! It's a way to sell that isn't scary or pushy; it's super effective, and it feels amazing. So first, let's talk about what sales is *not*. Sales is not manipulation. We are not here to manipulate someone into buying something that they don't need or that is not of value to them. So let's not say that we hate sales; let's say we don't like the actions of people who don't have the best interests of the client at heart. Sales has really gotten a bad reputation, and I'm not sure if we should blame the snake oil salesman or the used-car salesman. But as much as we all *love* to buy things, you'd think that a sales job would be put up on a pedestal as the awesome gatekeeper to all the stuff we want. (Insert star-eyed emoji here!)

How many times have you heard someone say, "Oh, I could never be in sales"? I hear that one all the time. "I could never do what you do" or "I'm not good at selling" are other common phrases. What they don't realize is the fact that selling is a part of life. It's *everywhere*, but many people miss it. For example, it's common knowledge that people who go into the entertainment industry hear the word "no" all the time, so they have to develop thick skin. If you think about it, they're selling their talent. They are selling their skills. But here's the truth: Every job in the world requires selling!

If you're a doctor, how do you get patients? You don't just graduate one day and suddenly your schedule is full. You have to sell yourself to other doctors to get into the office you want to work in, and you have to sell yourself to the patients, or they won't come back. If patients don't like your bedside manner, or if they don't think you have the knowledge or the skills they're looking for... *next*. My dentist hounds me every six months because we should all get our teeth cleaned twice a year— *aaand* because he has bills to pay. Let's be real. Come to think of it, whose idea was it that teeth need professional cleaning every six months? I'll bet it was a dentist.

"But Shari, hairdressers don't sell!" You *betcha* they do. You have to give a great haircut, sell products, and provide great customer service, or you will never see that person's head of hair again. Even our waiter tries to sell us on appetizers and desserts. I was *blown away* when my waiter friends told me that they were rated on their average ticket sale. "Sale? But it's not a sale; it's dinner." Oh, how naive I was! Turns out the waiters with the highest bill/ticket average are given the busiest shifts because they make the most money selling food for the restaurant. If you didn't know that, join the club. I'm sorry to tell you that you will never be the same. So now I feel guilty and worry about the waiter's job whenever I don't order appies and dessert. #fineIwillorderdessert #Ihelppeople

We sell ourselves at interviews for jobs, and we sell ourselves when we are out on dates. (Not *literally*! That is illegal. Stop it.) We sell ourselves to the in-laws and even to the other parents at park playdates. And yet when someone comes at us with a sample or a product as we are walking through the mall, we cringe and run away. (Is it just me? I actually do really hate that one.) #seriouslydudedo*not*comenearme

A funny thing happens when you work in retail sales. You hear "no" so much that it becomes almost meaningless. I would say hello to people, and they would respond with "no." Ummm... I was just saying hello. I was dumbfounded. You don't like hello? They weren't even listening. This is when it really hit me that the "no" wasn't personal. They didn't even see me! I could have been anybody. Two out of ten would listen, so I moved past the eight "no" sayers as quickly as possible. I was searching for the two who would listen. I sifted and sorted through my pile of "no"s until I found the "yes." I didn't take the "no"s personally; they just simply weren't my people. Moving rapidly past that which was not for me became an important theme in my life.

I LEFT the sales and management field back in 1996 to become a massage therapist. I thought that would be the opposite of sales, and I was all for it! I very quickly realized that to get the job at the spa, and to get clients, I had to sell my skills. I was single and self-employed, and if I didn't hustle and find clients, I was going to be single, self-employed, homeless, and starving! There was no option; I had to make it happen and risk hearing all the "no"s. (Insert big facepalm here when I realized I couldn't escape "the sell.")

There's a reason your hairdresser, massage therapist, esthetician, and so on want to "get you in the books for next time" before you leave your appointment. It's because there's a better chance of you rebooking if they can make it happen before you've left the building. I could fill my massage calendar two

Ask questions, find common ground, and then elevate the customer to understand the benefits of your products.

to three months in advance by telling my clients that I was booking out that far, when really my calendar was empty. But it ended up being a self-fulfilling prophecy because as they booked, I then actually became booked two to three months out. I had less chance of hearing "no" when they felt like appointments were scarce.

Remember Melinda from chapter 6? The woman who had her privacy settings shut down tight? Well, another reason she wasn't putting herself out there was because she was afraid of hearing the word "no." Welcome to the club, sister! I asked her how hearing the word "no" made her feel. It can mean different things to different people, and to Melinda, "no" meant "you're ridiculous." It was full of embarrassment and vulnerability for her. Many of you are probably nodding your head because you feel the same way. I totally get it. But here's the thing— that interpretation makes it about you. And it's not about *you*. It's about *your customer*. It's about coming from a place of service, helping people, finding pain points, and solving problems. Whether you're doing that through the products you sell or through the opportunity your business can provide for someone who needs extra income, you have something super special! *Own it!*

I asked Melinda, "What was one of your favorite jobs?" Turns out that when she was in college, she had waited tables to pay the bills. "I loved being around people," she said, "and I made great tips." I was not surprised because she was very friendly and personable. "It was a job that just came naturally to me. And it felt good bringing people their food, taking care of them, and making them happy." I was secretly jumping up and down inside because I knew we had just cracked the selling code for Melinda, and I couldn't wait to share it with her. Because words don't teach, it was time to lead her down the path toward selling enlightenment! #dramaticmuch?

I said, "So, let me get this straight. People would come to the restaurant because they were hungry, place their order with you, and then you'd give them what they'd ordered, and they would be happy. And that pleased you?" She looked at me like I was an idiot! Lol. She didn't realize where I was going with this just yet. Time to lower the boom. "How did the people know what sort of food to order?" Again with the blank stare. I could literally hear her blinking! Lol. She was probably regretting her life choices at this point and wondering why she ever decided to join my team. But I was about to make a *big point*, and then *all* would be revealed. Melinda said, "They looked at the menu!" I knew the "duh" was implied here. *Bazinga!* Three points! Nothing but net, baby! I was whooping and hollering, and she still didn't get it. *Oops.* Sorry, Mel. Got a little ahead of myself. Let me break it down:

1   Someone had a need. (They were hungry.)

2   They knew, generally, the sort of things you had to offer. (Restaurants have food.)

3   They looked at the list of what specific things you could provide. (The menu.)

4   They ordered. (*Psst. Has *nothing* to do with you. It's about *them*.)

"So, it's exactly what you do now with your current business," I said. Think about it:

1   Someone has a need. (Your products can provide a solution.)

2   By talking about this need on social media, customers will know what you have to offer.

3   Your website is the menu.

4   They order. (One more time for the people in the back: *It is not about yooouuu!*)

If a customer comes into the restaurant, looks at the menu, and decides to just order a cup of tea, or decides there isn't anything on the menu that looks appetizing to her at that moment, so she leaves—does that mean she hates you? Should you be embarrassed by the menu? Will you still offer that same menu to other people? Is that a sign that you should quit your job? Absolutely not, because you know that it's not personal. "No" isn't personal. If a customer says no, then they simply don't need what you are offering, *or* you haven't yet established that need. They may not yet have realized that they need your product.

Melinda's mouth dropped open. She just stared at me, and I could see the clouds parting as the realization hit her. I waited with excitement, trying to squelch the 12-year-old little-girl squeal that was bubbling up inside me as I watched it dawn on her that she was simply looking at the situation from the wrong angle. Her real-time words were, "What in the actual hell. All this time I was telling myself a story and making sales something it didn't have to be." *That*, my friend, is a False Truth. It was a thought that she continued to think, so she believed it. She changed the thought, so she changed the belief! I shall neither confirm nor deny that at that moment, I did a victory dance that included the moonwalk with a side of Cabbage Patch. #fistbump #dothehustle

When Melinda took some time to identify the feelings the word "no" gave her, she could defuse them. I asked her, "Have you ever said no to someone?"

Well, of course she had.

I said, "Okay, so when you said no to someone, was that because they were a ridiculous fool?"

"No. I just wasn't interested, or it wasn't a good time," she said.

"Okay, so it had nothing to do with the person?"

"No."

"Have you ever said no to a friend but still liked them?"

She got the point loud and clear.

Melinda's story is ultimately about freedom. She freed herself from the fears and false truths that were holding her back. What makes me proudest is watching how she has blossomed into a leader who now helps others break through their fears. What makes her the *best* coach is that she had to walk through that same fire, so she knows how to lead the way. Embrace your challenges—because they are here to make you a better version of yourself!

From Salesperson to Problem Solver

I'm sure that at some time in your young life, you were involved with a fundraiser for your school or team and had to sell cookies, candy, or popcorn to your friends and family. If your mama was hardcore, and *smart*, she made you go door to door. I did this to *myself*, believe it or not. When I was eight years old, I wanted a camera. My little neighbor friend, whom we called "Poohie" (don't ask), had this catalog, and she told me that if we sold the greeting cards and wrapping paper in it, we could earn a camera as a prize. It was an Instamatic with the flashcubes, and it was all the rage in 1978. Ladies and gentlemen, I believe this is where my selling education began. I took my little bowl-cut-hairdo self, my corduroy slacks, and my Buster Brown shoes, and I hit the pavement!

I remember going door to door, scared to death that someone would answer. Yikes. And then what would I say? Reliving this experience, I realize with horror that back in the seventies, we didn't think twice about going into a stranger's home to sit on the couch while they smoked a cig and looked over the catalog. I think back and just shake my head. It's a miracle that we all survived. Maybe I thought it was okay because it was such a small town, and we knew everyone—but still! Well, dang it, I wanted that camera, so common sense be damned! And guess what? I earned it!

I remember the door slamming in my face so many times. Sometimes I didn't even have a chance to say hello before they shut the door. It went something like this:

"Hello—" Door slams shut.

Blink, blink.

Next house: "Hello—"

"No thanks, kid."

Next house: "Hi, I'm Sh—"

"Not interested."

Hmph.

Okay, I was running out of houses—as I mentioned, it was a small town. I was quickly learning that leading with my name was wasting time because they weren't hearing my offer. Each time it would definitely sting, but it would also cause me to rethink my sales pitch. I'd hone it and twist it, and I'd work to get the key words out before that door slammed. I decided that my name could wait; I had to get to the point of it, so my sales pitch morphed into something like:

"Would you like—"

"No thanks."

Next house: "I am selling—"

"Not interested."

Ugh!! I was not giving up! But in remembering this story, I really had to think about what it was that pushed me to continue, besides the camera, because being so young and going through that much rejection should have made me stop and give up on the whole idea! I realized that it was because at eight years old, I thought every adult knew how to sell—how to pitch a product and talk to people. I thought of it as something that I had to learn, so I figured I might as well start right then. I never even considered that I had the option to just say no and not learn new things. Learn it now or learn it later. I had it in my head that by the time I was an adult, I had to learn how to do adult things, and that was just the way it was. I thought it was normal that kids didn't know how to sell and were nervous, but adults weren't scared because they had already learned how. This was just my time to learn!

The final tweak that cracked the code to keeping the doors from slamming shut was this: I would simply say, with enthusiasm, "Greeting cards!" and that got their attention! (Also, I find that enthusiasm stuns people for a hot minute while they're figuring out why you're so excited.) My follow-up was, "Have you ever wanted to send someone a birthday card, but you didn't have one handy?" Aha! They were listening... and thinking. So I would quickly add: "I have wrapping paper too."

Sold! I now know that I had hit a pain point—I'd solved a problem and made their life easier. Win-win. It's always got to be a win-win. Always. You thrive when you find solutions to people's problems. To me, this is the most fulfilling part about selling, and it's what keeps me going and thriving. This lesson is what I most want to impart to you. What you do matters! Sales *matters* when you put the customer's needs first. You are allowed to make a living helping other people solve problems, y'know? We make fun of "used-car salesmen" for a reason— because we know that's not how it's supposed to be done. It feels gross, so you are not wrong for feeling nauseous at the thought of operating your business that way. Trust your gut! It's telling you to find a better way. It's time to focus on things that provide you with *fulfillment*, which is not the same as happiness.

As we talked about in chapter 2, happiness is short-lived. Happiness is the promotion that gives you a thrill for a week, or the sale that gives you a thrill for a day. Fulfillment lasts forever.

Their bank statement
is none of your business!
**Everyone deserves
your best service.**

It's knowing you did something good that helped someone else. That can never be taken away from you, and it's something that stays with you. It's what puts purpose into your everyday actions. At the age of eight, I went from being a seller to being a helper. It wasn't about me; it was about them. And hey, if a second grader can learn to do it, so can you.

The art of non-selling is rooted in honesty and integrity. When I'm coaching, I reinforce the fact that selling doesn't have to be slimy! In fact, it *shouldn't* be slimy! (Insert deep breath here.) So just imagine how it would feel if you sold your products and services the way that *you* would want to be sold to, in a way that doesn't make you feel like you're taking advantage of anyone. *That* is the goal! Most people are shoppers at heart. We all have things that we would love to have, and we need a salesperson to give us the correct info about them. So be the information booth. Tell them the features and benefits of what you are offering. Find their pain point and provide a solution. It's not a hit to your ego if they don't buy what you're selling. If it's not for them, it's not for them, and that's okay! Don't make it about you.

The Art of Non-selling in Action

Let's say you have a favorite nail polish brand. It's your all-time fave because it doesn't chip, and your manicure lasts for two whole weeks. Have you told your BFF about it? Your mom? Your sister? Anyone who comments on your nails or on their own nails, or anytime a nail comes up in conversation? I bet you can't shut up about the products you love! That, my friend, is what I'm talking about. We can go on and on about our favorite things—until we begin earning money on those things.

"Well, Shari, I can't possibly talk about that now. They will think I just want their money." *Do* you just want their money? If the answer is no, then you, my dear friend, are your own problem. You need to tell yourself a different story. The fact is, you don't know what they are thinking. If you have a relationship with them, then they should know you and know that you aren't sleazy like that. If you do *not* have a relationship with them, carry on and be your true, authentic self. As you are building their trust, they will see by your actions, attitude, and confidence that you truly believe in what you're selling. If I love my nail polish, does that mean you must love my nail polish as much as I do, or else I'm a liar and a cheat? Heavens no! Share what you love, and people will decide for themselves. Now, how many of you are still wondering about the name of my polish? #muahaha #artofnonsellinginactionbaby #oliveandjune

Remember—if your mouth is closed, so is your business. Stop hesitating with your business, because when you are hesitant, you look like you are not confident in what you are selling. You may be hesitant because in your head you're afraid that someone is thinking, "She just wants my money," or "Who is she to recommend these products?" But you *don't* know what they are thinking, and honestly, chances are that they aren't thinking about you at all. There's an old saying: "When you're 20, you care what everyone thinks. When you're 40, you stop caring what everyone thinks. When you're 60, you realize no one was ever thinking about you in the first place." The last line is the truth. Nobody is thinking about you and judging you even *half* as much as you are thinking about and judging yourself. So stop it! #mamasays

I MET Jessica in 2018. She had struggled with selling for years before we began working together. Try as she might, she just could never seem to sell. She changed her wording, and she changed companies, but it all boiled down to Jessica. She was desperate to find answers, and that was her problem. Desperation. It was written all over her, with a side helping of defeat.

First things first, we had to ditch that baggage. The way you carry yourself is everything, and el desperado isn't a good look on anyone.

This is how Jessica would approach her customers: "Hey, Gwen. How are you? Listen, I have this really great product, and if you'd be willing to post about it on social media for me, I can give you one for free. But if you're busy, I totally understand."

Hmm . . . lackluster at best. Right off the bat, she was offering something for free, which sends the message that she's desperate, that her product isn't worth much, and that she's willing to give it away for free as a bribe because she's got nothing else going on. Nope, nope, nope! We both decided she could do better! So we brainstormed and created a new story and persona for her. We wrote it as if it were her introduction onto a grand stage to speak about her accomplishments, and it went something like this:

> Jessica is an extremely successful business builder with a huge team. She loves her products and loves helping others find solutions! She wakes up every day with a skip in her step and a list of people who want what she's selling. She has so many customers, and the list continues to grow! She has people joining her team daily, and that keeps her pretty busy with training, but she still loves making time to share these wonderful products because she knows others will love them as much as she does.

Okay, so that's Jessica 2.0. I asked current Jessica how she thought Jessica 2.0 would present herself to the world, having such a big, bustling business? Her entire being changed, right down to her posture and even her tone of voice. She sat up straighter, cleared her throat, and with a much bolder voice, said, "Well, if I had a big business, I would be confident. I would be *calm* and happy, eager to help people, and not afraid of rejection because I already had so many other customers." #tellherwhatsheswonBob

Next, I asked, "How would Jessica 2.0 approach a customer?"

She thought for a moment and said, "She would talk to the customer in a straightforward, friendly way, like she's talking to a good friend. Something like, 'Hey, Kathy. Next time you need mascara, you have to try this. Hope you're well!'" *Boom-shakalakalaka, baby.*

I seriously needed to take a moment after that one. *Wow.* Did she completely change who she was? Not really. She simply came from a different place inside herself—a place we all have, but we just sometimes forget. So here is your wake-up call! *You* have amazing things inside you, and a gift that only *you* can give to the world by being your strong, confident self. It's time to wake up and show up as that part of yourself every day. Practice makes progress, and you (and the world) deserve every bit of what that confident you has to offer. #grouphug

This sort of confident approach falls right in line with the art of non-selling because it's putting the offering—the "menu"—on the table. It's not a slick or sleazy sale, and it's also not pushy. It treats the customer with respect, by getting right to the point and leaving the rest of the pleasantries to the end. When you reach out to someone and put a bunch of pretense first, the entire time, they are most likely thinking, "Hmm... what does she want?" Like Simon Sinek taught us, hit them with it right up front, and then the rest of your comments will be better received!

You Are the Product, Baby!

A beautiful thing happens when you come from a place of service, remain authentic, and put the customer first. The relationship between you and your customer grows. Your reputation grows. Your confidence grows. And then, *exponentially*, all three of those things flourish and feed into one another. You form friendships with your customers, and then they tell their friends, spreading your great reputation, which then makes you feel even more confident in your business and your ability to help others, and the cycle repeats.

Have you ever gone into a store knowing what you needed, and yet you still ended up walking out because the salesperson was sleazy or desperate or rude? I have! We buy people, not just products. If someone likes you and trusts you, it doesn't matter *what* you're selling; they will buy it. The key is to put the customer *first*. Find a need or a problem that they have, and then help them solve it.

> **HOT TIP!** Don't try to trick or to manipulate your customers. They know what they like and what they want, so just tell them what you're offering and respect their ability to decide for themselves. If you are desperate, your customers can smell it a mile away. If you just want to make a buck and don't really care about their needs, they will know. In that case, you've lost before you've even started. They will not be buying *you* as a person, so for *sure* they're not going to buy anything that you're selling.

Sometimes what you have to offer doesn't solve their problem. What then? Integrity and honesty are king! If you don't have something that solves their problem, help them find the solution anyway—even if that means going beyond your company's products. The relationship and trust between you and your customer is priceless. It needs to thrive above all else. Just imagine how much trust you will build with that customer if you are honest and say that you don't currently have anything that would solve their problem, but you're going to help them look for something that will. The goal isn't that one sale. The goal is the relationship and their trust. Because if you're suggesting something that isn't what they need, they won't enjoy that product anyway. And it's okay if you don't know *for sure* that your product will help them. But be honest and say something like, "Okay, Karen, I have this product that does xyz, and I think it might help. Why don't you try it and keep me posted? If it's not working, I want to know." Let her know that you are her advocate and will do whatever you can to make it right.

It's been my experience that when a customer knows you're on their side, even if they aren't totally in love with the product, they are less likely to return it—because they like *you*. Back when I worked for a department store cosmetic company, if I didn't have what the customer needed, I would walk around the department to other cosmetic counters and help my customer find something that would work. I promise you, that customer was *my* customer for life. So much so that when I switched cosmetic companies and customers would see me at a different counter wearing a different coat, they would say, "Shari, you're over here now? Okay, what do I need?" Can you imagine the sort of business you could build if that was the attitude of your customers? They trust *me*; they are buying *me*, because they know I will put their best interests first. This is the sort of culture you want to create within your business, where *you* are the commodity, and the product is secondary. And when someone gets great service from someone whom they like, guess what they do? They *tell their friends*! #lookatyoumakingfriends #mamaissoproud

As you grow and develop your relationships, think of the art of non-selling as a tool to help you reframe who you're selling to. Think of the continuing relationship as *the* most important thing. No sale is greater than your relationship with your customer, and when you practice, you're going to see yourself moving those relationships to the next level. #yougrowgirl

"Price is what you pay, **value is what you get.**"

WARREN BUFFETT

Probe, Align, and Raise

. . . .

It's so interesting to me when I hear women get down on themselves for not being able to sell. I always ask them how many
classes they've taken on selling, or how many books they've
read. Most often the answer is zero! Okay, then how can you
expect to know how to do something if you've never been
taught? On-the-job training is the best teacher, but most people hear the word "no" a few times and they stop trying. Let me
teach you one of the best tips I know on how to sell effectively
and give your customer the best, most thoughtful customer
service. These three words—probe, align and raise—are game
changers for your business. It's so simple!

Probe

Ask questions. Find your customer's pain points. What are their
issues, and what do they want to improve? "Jennifer, if you
could improve anything about your [skin/health/makeup/hair
or whatever product you sell], what would it be?" Or "Jennifer,
what would you say is your biggest issue with your skin/health/
makeup/hair?"

Align

Let your customer know that you understand what they are saying, and that you've heard them. Mirror back to them. Example:
"Okay, so your biggest concern is with xyz?" or, "Okay, so what
I'm hearing is that if you could eliminate/improve xyz, that
would be amazing."

Raise

Take your customer to the next level. You've met her where
she's at by probing and aligning. You know what her concerns
are, and she knows that you understand, so now you raise: "Let

me show you what I have to improve your [insert the concern here]." Give her some proof, such as your personal experience or statements on your company's website, maybe a few testimonials. If you don't have the same issue that she does, do not worry! You don't have to have the same concerns as your customer to be of value to her. You can say, "This product [insert name] helps [give claims from website]" and/or "My friend [insert friend's name] swears by it! It has really helped her with [insert similar condition]."

Don't be afraid to recommend all the products that would best help your customer. Here's how I like to do it: "Jennifer, you said your biggest concern is fine lines and wrinkles, and so I'm going to show you the products that will help you with that." I give her the list, and let's say there are four products. (Don't faint; stay with me.) I explain to her what each product does and why it's important. Then I say, "If you purchased all four today, your total would be xyz."

Wait to see what she says. Basically, shut it! You are the waiter; it's her decision. You don't know how desperate she is to correct her issues or how long she's been struggling. If she says she can't afford all the items at once, you can say, "I totally understand. Okay, let's get you the most important ones first, and you can add the others as your budget allows. I'd start with x and y because [give her the reasons]. Would that work?" Let her decide. No matter what she says, you can say, "Great! This is a terrific start for you, and I know you're going to love it. I'll write down the other items I recommended for you so we don't forget. Then you can just let me know when you're ready for them." Then, remember to do the Five Steps to Follow-up that we discussed in chapter 7.

That is great customer service. It's not icky or gross; it's *service*!

Get Out of Her Wallet

. . . .

Well, this is embarrassing. Want to hear a story about the time
I was a judgmental jerk? Yeah, I figured. #spillthetea So there
I was, 23 years old, finishing up my last year in college, working behind the Estée Lauder counter. I had a customer come
up to the counter looking very disheveled. Her hair was falling
out of a messy bun, and she was wearing a T-shirt and ripped
jeans, back before ripped jeans were cool. She had a few little
kids with her and was pushing an empty stroller. She needed a
moisturizer, and we had an *amazing* new one, but it was *really*
expensive. I felt bad for the customer because I could tell that
she couldn't afford it, so I didn't even mention it. Instead, I recommended another less expensive moisturizer that was good,
just not as good as the new one. We finished up the sale, and I
was feeling like I had just done a good deed, looking out for the
best interests of this poor woman. I was a *good, kind* salesperson [pats self on the back].

Here's where it went sideways—as soon as I hand the pack-
age over to my customer, another woman comes around the
corner carrying a baby and puts her in the stroller. Then she
hands my customer a Louis Vuitton purse. Sooo, this new lady
was the *nanny*. She had taken my customer's $3,000 handbag
with her to go to the car and change the baby's diaper. So obviously, I judged a book by its cover, but wait—it gets worse. As
my customer started to walk away, something caught her eye
at the next counter. I heard the consultant asking her lots of
questions about her skin. Let me just cut to the chase of this
painful moment: Because the other consultant focused on the
needs of the customer and not on what she *assumed* was in the
woman's bank account, she gave this woman exceptional customer service by suggesting products that would give her the
best skin possible. Cleansers, toners, serums, eye cream, masks,

the works! The final total was over $500, and I watched my $35 customer walk away with the biggest smile on her face, thanking the other consultant profusely for her help. Seriously? Well, that's what I got for—being judgy! And for all I know, she was a fashion icon or a trendsetter with the very first pair of ripped jeans.

I've gotten a ton of mileage out of that lesson, so I'm grateful for the experience. It obviously made an indelible mark upon my psyche. *Never again* would I assume what was in someone's wallet, and neither should you! #nunyabusiness For all we know, a customer could have been saving birthday money and Christmas money for years and was finally ready to make a purchase. So the question is, "Are you going to give her the best advice you can give, or are you going to hold back out of fear?" The customer doesn't know what you have to offer unless you show her. What she decides to do with the information is up to *her* and has *zero* to do with you!

Sharing Is Caring

When you have a great experience at a restaurant or a store, or when you find a product that you *love*, do you share it? Most of us do! But then this weird thing happens when we start selling something that we love. We freeze! I find it interesting that people are very eager to share their love of a product with the world... until they are making money off that product. Then they get in their head: "Oh, I can't share this because people are going to think I just want their money." Is that true, or is it a product that you love, and it just so happens that customers can get that product through you? I would like to think that people are selling the products *because* they love them so much!

Elizabeth was that go-to person for her friends who was always recommending things. You know the type. Heck, maybe you *are* the type! When you find something that you love, no matter what it is, you gotta tell everyone about it! But a funny thing happened on the way to building her business. Elizabeth could talk about the products she loved all day long *until* she started earning money on them. It was like someone put a wet blanket on her. Her entire demeanor changed! Where did that bubbly, energetic personality go? I've seen this scenario a million times, so I knew it was time to dig into the story Elizabeth was telling herself. Just as I suspected, she was telling herself that people were going to think she just wanted their money. Here's what is so beautiful about the social media world that we live in today—you can go *live* and actually talk to people and explain the who, what, and why of your product, and eliminate all doubt! You can provide value by sharing what issues your products solved for you. Who doesn't love a good recommendation from someone they know and trust?

If you think you have to manipulate people into buying, you will fail. This isn't the way to build a business, much less a business that you can be proud of. There is tremendous joy in being able to help others solve a problem, and one thing I've learned over the years is that if *you* have a problem, someone else does too! We all have more similarities than differences, and talking about the solutions you've discovered will make you very relatable.

Once we figured out the story Elizabeth was telling herself, we planned for her to go live to share what these products had done for her, talking like she would to her best friends. She found her energy again and realized that her hang-ups were all in her head! She *did* believe in her products, and there's nothing wrong with having a job where you get paid for recommmending things that have worked for you and people you know. In fact, it's silly not to! There's no reason you need to be free advertisement for a company. You and your referrals are worth the commission you're paid!

Ultimately, the "art of non-selling" is asking you to forget what you've experienced from most salespeople in the past and just be yourself. Be the kind, caring person you are. You are a gift to your customers because you care, and they can feel safe in knowing they have a partner who puts their needs first and helps them solve their problems. You are the information booth, the waitress, and you show them everything that you have to offer. Give them the respect of allowing them to decide for themselves. When you approach your business in this way, you *cannot* fail. You and your customer both win, and that is the only way it should ever be!

Here's an exercise: When was the last time you took 15 minutes of quiet time with a pen and paper to write down your fears and identify why you're afraid? Let's journal for a few minutes.

- What scares you about growing a business? Where does that fear come from?

- What would it mean for your business if you were to do the thing that you were most afraid of?

- Think back to Jessica. What would the 2.0 version of you look like? How would she show up to the world? How would she approach people, and what would she say?

- What are two small steps you could take to get you going in the *direction* of your goal *today*?

I guarantee that the thing you're afraid of is primarily just a belief that isn't 100% true!

9

Duplication Nation! How to Build a Business

It doesn't matter what works,
it matters what duplicates.
OLIVER BURMAN

Hocus-Pocus, Let's Stay Focused!

A few months into my network marketing business, I had a great idea. What if I joined a second company and became the "one-stop shop" for my customers? They could get everything they needed from me! I thought I was a genius. I bet nobody else had ever thought of that. #everyonehasthoughtofthat Well, I was only a few weeks into my second business when I had a massive realization: The time it was taking me to get that other business rolling was *taking away* from my original business. Not only that, but I found myself with a daily dilemma: Do I post about the first company or the second? Which products do I offer to my potential customers? Which business opportunity do I offer?

The truth is that your customer only has so much disposable income. Let's say they have $100 to spend. Is it more beneficial that they spend $100 with one of your businesses or divide that amount between two businesses? You will grow and promote faster if all $100 goes toward one business. I realized that I could have one *awesome* thriving business or two mediocre businesses. Needless to say, I ditched that second business like a hot potato. I could see quickly in that first couple of weeks that my momentum in my first business was slowing, and it was holding me back.

Remember that if you have time to run a second business, you aren't working your first business to its full potential. You won't find a top leader in any network marketing company who is running two businesses and staying at the top—because it is not possible. Now, that doesn't mean you can't become an affiliate for a product that doesn't compete with your company. But you absolutely can't run two network marketing businesses and be at the top! You can't be a successful lawyer and a successful doctor at the same time. You need to decide. If you want to be at the top, put all your eggs in one basket, and stay focused on that basket! If you have extra time on your hands, enjoy it, and/or find other activities you can do to continue growing your business.

I see this same situation happen over and over again, and just like me, these women all think they've had a genius idea. I hate to be the party pooper, my friend, but I have seen this hundreds of times, and it never ends well. I know that often words don't teach, so some of you may need to experience it for yourself. But if you want to save time and energy, listen to Mama! Pour 100% of your heart and soul into one business. Don't divide your time and energy. As I said, you can have one *incredible* business or two mediocre ones. The work is the same; the money is different.

If your energy and focus are divided, you can only go so far. If all your energy is focused in one direction, you can grow exponentially! It's as simple as that. And multitasking will lead to quicker burnout because you are burning the candle at both ends.

Trish went through something similar. She wanted to be the one-stop shop for her customers. She felt like it was the way to go, and nothing I said could convince her otherwise. This was a moment as a leader when I had to just step back and let Trish figure it out for herself. She was fired up with tons of enthusiasm and excitement, so that was a great start! She started hosting home parties to showcase the makeup and jewelry that she was selling, as well as posting on her social media. She was working two jobs, trying to get them both off the ground, and

If you divide your time, you divide your income.

it was a few months later when she came back to me, worn out and deflated. She didn't understand why she couldn't make much ground in either business, so she felt like maybe sales wasn't the business for her.

As much as I hated to see her so down, I could tell that she was more open to suggestions and more coachable now that she had some experience working both businesses. All it took was pointing out to her that if she added up the sales from her makeup business and her jewelry business, that grand total could have come from just one business. She could literally have doubled one of her businesses. We looked at her social media and counted how many posts she made for each business, and if she added those together and had posted that many times for one business, she could have doubled her exposure. You just can't drive two cars and expect to go as far as you would driving one. #seriouslypullover Not to mention that once you've hit a leadership level, most network marketing businesses will not allow you to work two companies, so pick a lane from the get-go.

Basic Duplication

In chapter 7, you learned how to build your business by doing a few simple things:

- Getting the hero product into the hands of as many people as possible.

- Asking your five closest friends to host an online event, introducing you to approximately 25 new people each (125 people in total).

- Booking five more online events from those 125 people.

Well, guess what? The most effective way to *duplicate* your efforts is to teach others how to do those same three things. And then they teach their team, and so on and so on! It really is that simple, and the simpler you can make it, the more people are likely to do it, so the more effective it will be!

If you want to build a business and build a team, it doesn't matter what *you* can do personally as much as it matters what you can *duplicate*. You could be an amazing seller, photogenic, great at selfies, and have a giant following on social media, but if your new person can't do what you do, you won't be able to grow a team. If you keep it simple, it won't be intimidating or overwhelming, and your team will be more likely to get into action! Constantly ask yourself: "Is my system of sharing products on social media something that anyone and everyone can do?" If not, break the steps down even further. It's important to make things as simple as possible, but making things simple isn't always easy!

Making things simple for others, so that it's duplicatable, doesn't mean that you have to stop doing fancy things, such as creating videos or tutorials, especially if you love doing that. Just make it clear to your team that you don't expect them to start where you're at currently. We all start from square one. Your hero product is the gateway! When people try it and love it, during the course of your follow-up, they will likely say, "That was great! What else do you have?" And then you're off to the races!

There are a million and one ways to grow a business, so if you've found a way to grow that is different from what I've suggested, *girl*, you go with your bad self! #yasqueen But if you need guidance, I will tell you that the most important thing is to be authentic and master the basics that I listed on the previous page.

Warning! One of the biggest challenges I often see when someone is growing and adding people to their team is that they will suddenly stop selling and working their personal business because they are attending to the new people on the team. Do *not* slow your roll, sister! You need to keep up your sales, so invite your new people to shadow you and do what you're doing.

Let them mirror you! It's the best, simplest way to keep your momentum and train them at the same time. Here's how I like to describe it: Picture yourself running around the track at your high school. You are running that track and making great time! You see some people standing on the sidelines watching you, so as you pass them, you invite them to run with you. As more and more people start running with you, you suddenly stop to turn around and see what they are doing. When you stop, they stop. Now you are all looking at one another, and nobody is moving. This is bad for business! *Do not stop!*

Instead, you run ... they run. You say, "Look what I'm doing here! Try it!" They try it. Some will and some won't. Focus on those who try it. The ones who don't? Love them where they're at, but don't spend time trying to drag them across the finish line. They know where you are when they are ready. Remember that 20% of your team will do 80% of the sales. You are one person, and you only have so much time in a day, so spend it wisely!

> **HOT TIP!** If you find yourself worried about what your team is *not* doing, ask yourself, "What am *I* doing to move business forward?" The more *you* do, the less you worry about others.

I've got a million analogies, in case you haven't noticed, but when it comes to my team, I think of communication as a tennis match. For example, I will message them with some tips or coaching advice for their business. If they get back to me with questions, I will get back to them with another tip for the next step. And so it goes. But when they stop, I stop. I spent way too many years being more concerned about someone else's business than they were themselves. I learned the hard way that we need to meet people where they're at. If you have questions for me or want to take it to the next level, I'm here for it! But I refuse to feel more responsible for someone's success than they do.

Four-Week Flow

I noticed in the first few months of my network marketing business that in the last few days of the month, I would push myself to hit a goal or promotion and wake up on the first of the next month completely exhausted. So there I was at zero dollars on the first of the month, with no energy to start over. I knew I had to find a way to change that, because it was mentally draining to constantly feel like I was starting over every month. So I decided the best way to do that was to "front-load" the month. I got that phrase from my kids' pediatrician, when I was concerned that my daughter wasn't eating much at lunch and dinner. The pediatrician asked me what she ate for breakfast, and I told her, "A waffle, scrambled eggs, sausage, bacon, and a banana." I'll never forget the way she stared at me, not speaking for what felt like forever. "Umm, Mrs. Brown, your daughter is a front-loader. She eats the bulk of her calories in the morning, so I wouldn't worry about what she eats the rest of the day." It's true—she ate her breakfast like a lumberjack! Lol.

But this "front-loader" idea came back to me when I realized that if I could start the month strong, I wouldn't have to kill myself at the end of every month to hit my goals. It was going to take some extra effort in the very beginning to get myself up and moving when the month began, but if I did that one time, I could alter the cycle of my business. No more late nights closing out the month! Hallelujah! This is where the Four-Week Flow was born.

The Four-Week Flow is a simple system that helps you end one month strong *and* carry that momentum into the following month to start strong. What does this look like? Let's look at an example, using March and April and a ten-day event. A ten-day event might sound intimidating, but really, it's just posting once or twice a day about your products, sharing videos and information, and going live every few days if you can. If you're not yet up to going live, that's okay. Baby steps! You can still post content and be effective. In the example below, you will do two rounds of online events, one in the last week of March and one in the second week of April, following up in Weeks 1 and 3, like this:

- Week 4 of March (approx. March 25 to April 4): Begin online event

- Week 1 of April (April 5–9): Follow up with customers and prep for next event

- Week 2 of April (April 10–19): Begin online event

- Week 3 of April (April 20–24): Follow up with customers and prep for next event

- Week 4 of April (April 25 to May 4): Begin online event

(Notice that Week 4 in March and Weeks 2 and 4 in April are the same! Weeks 1 and 3 are also the same.)

And we begin again. Rinse and repeat.

Let's talk more about the fourth week of the month. This is when you'll want to start your event. (More on how to do that in a minute.) Depending on how long your event will be, you'll want the last half or at least one-third of it to carry over into the next month. I'd recommend seven to ten days for your event, not five days, because your customers won't see all of your posts in only five days. Seven to ten days will guarantee that they see at least four days of posts. Most events get the bulk of their sales in the final few days because by then your audience has been exposed to more of your posts and lives. Make sure you don't take your foot off the gas, even if you're not seeing sales in the first several days. This is *totally normal* and should be expected! If you have been consistent, the final two days should be your biggest sales days. And remember, the value of one of these events is not just the sales; it's the network!

Your audience has had seven to ten days of getting to know you, and that is invaluable! You are playing the long game here and developing trust with future clients, not just looking for a quick one-time sale.

Four-Week Flow Calendar (March/April)

SUN	MON	TUES	WED	THUR	FRI	SAT
25	26	27	28	29	30	31
1	2	3	4	5	6	7
8	9	10	11	12	13	14
15	16	17	18	19	20	21
22	23	24	25	26	27	28

March 25 to April 4: Begin online event
April 5–9: Follow up with customers and prep for next round
April 10–19: Begin Round 2 of online event
April 20–24: Follow up with customers and prep for next round
April 25 onward: Begin online event

In the Business of Networking

Remember, my friend, you are in the *networking* business, so the best way to build your network is—pardon the repetition—to network! Got it? Always be on the lookout for referrals. The best way to do this is to offer something of value before ever

If you have time to run
more than one business,
**you're not running either
one to its potential.**

seeking a sale. Do this through online parties, workshops, and tutorials, and help customers solve a problem with your products. When I do an online event, I like to create a private group on Facebook, one for each of my customers who are interested, and then I ask her to add at least 25 friends. It's nice if you send each of her friends a friend request and a private message saying something like:

> Hi, Stacy. I'm Shari, and Kathy Miller is our mutual friend. I wanted to let you know that Kathy added you to a group where I'll be doing some free [makeup/nutrition/jewelry—whatever you sell] tutorials for the next week! I don't like it when I'm added to a group and not told about it, so I wanted to let you know and introduce myself.

Make the message personal. The way I see it, if I want a customer to spend five minutes shopping on my website, then they deserve a few minutes of my time sending them a thoughtful message. These personal touches go a long way!

Post once or twice daily, and remember that going live is the best. Don't wait for anyone to hop on the live, though, because most will watch the replay. Just know what you want to say, and get right to it! Here are some examples:

- "Got tiny lashes? Watch what this mascara can do!"

- "Low energy? Take a look at this supplement!"

- "Tired of your wardrobe? Let me show you how this jewelry can jazz it up!"

If you've never done an online event before, you're probably "scared pea green and purple," as my grandma used to say! I have no idea where that phrase came from or what it really means, and yet . . . it fits. So *congratulations*—you're normal! Let's be scared and do it anyway, k? K. #youcanpunchmelater

Remember—when you're afraid to do something, break it down into bite-sized pieces, and make a plan.

When I'm nervous, I often think back to all the jobs I've had in my life where I had to do things that made me nervous and uncomfortable. #coldcallinganyone But I had to do it because it was my job. I'm sure you've had that experience once or thrice too, right?! If you would do it for someone else's business, then you need to do it for your *own* business! You won't be scared forever; I promise. It's just because it's new. Your first try won't be your best one, but each time you do it, you'll get better and better. Practice makes progress. And no matter what, don't forget to be proud of yourself for stepping up and taking the leap!

> **HOT TIP!** Considering the speed at which social media moves, here are some ideas to inspire you to find new ways to promote your products. Ever considered doing a class on TikTok, or Reels, or in your Stories? Maybe host an event on YouTube, and then share the link in a Messenger chat or in a group text or email? The opportunities are only limited by your imagination! New features are showing up all the time, so take advantage of them. Social media favors the early adopters of the newest features, so blaze that trail, sister!

The Sponsoring Lifestyle

If you want to grow a business, you need to grow a team. This is true with any business, not just network marketing. The bigger the number of lawyers, the bigger the law firm.

So how do you grow your team? I know you're probably expecting a giant chapter just on this subject, but it's not that complicated. Take everything you have learned so far about selling your product and apply it to selling the business opportunity!

- Make sure you're talking about it regularly.

- Share the benefits of it.

- Show all aspects of yourself on social media.

- Be your authentic self.

If you can sell a product, you can sell the business, but you've got to extend the invitation. Expect that there will be more customers who want to buy your products than people who want to build a business, and that's okay. I've found that if I incorporate my gratitude for what the business has done for me and my family into my conversations and social media posts, then building a team becomes effortless and very effective!

Don't hide the fact that you're looking for women who want to earn money from their phone and that you provide free training. Work on your ten-second answer when someone asks you what you do for a living. I always say, "I show women how to build a business from their phone." That is a sure way to get a response like, "Oh, wow. That's cool. What sort of business?" To which I reply, "You know how you see people all over social media sharing products that they love, and in return they earn commission?" They nod, and I say, "That's what I do!" #boomski Seed planted. You don't need to say any more than that unless they ask. Move on with the conversation, and don't think that you have to get them to sign up right there in the Target aisle. Sometimes as I say goodbye, I'll throw in, "Hey! If you or anyone you know is ever interested in learning how to make money online, let me know!" That's a call to action, baby.

If you planted seeds day after day, whenever the opportunity presented itself, you could have planted 20 seeds or more over the course of a month—and over the course of a year, that could be hundreds! Out of those hundreds, you might have a dozen or more who are interested. Those who aren't interested today might be interested next month or next year or in two years. I've had women watch me for years before they finally decided to join. Plant seeds as often as you can so that you never find yourself backed into a corner and desperate. Bees and dogs can smell fear... and so can your potential teammates!

Don't make sponsoring a thing that you sit down and check off your to-do list. Incorporate it into your life using the tips I gave you, but also by making friends in your real life as well as online. Do you know the name of your supermarket clerk, your barista, your mail carrier, your dog groomer, your neighbors, your manicurist? If not, you should! Consider looking for the same clerk every time you go to the store (and remember her name), or strike up a conversation with your neighbors while walking your dog. Be intentional about making new friends. Life is hard, so go spread some smiles and kindness! (Don't use the fact that you're an introvert as an excuse. Oh, I see you hiding over there! I'm an introvert too, so no excuses!) It's not just good for your business; it's good for your life. #putthenetworkinmarketing

10

Big Whoop!

That which is for you will not pass you.
SCOTTISH PROVERB

"**B**IG FREAKIN' whoop!" This is my go-to response when life hands me lemons, especially in business. It does two things for me: First, it lifts the heaviness and fear from a situation, reminding me that I have complete power over my attitude and point of view. Second, it reminds me that "everything is figureoutable," as Marie Forleo says in her book of the same name.

Back order? Big whoop! Here's my pivot: "This is a very popular product, so place your order ASAP!" Out of stock? Big whoop! Pivot: "That product *flew* out the door! I'll let you know when it's back in stock, but in the meantime, check out this product." Customer doesn't like your product? Big whoop! You've got lots of products to offer, and not everyone will enjoy them all. A team member quit? Big whoop! Have you had more than one job in your lifetime? People leave jobs every day, and you don't want someone whose heart isn't in the business. Give your time and energy to those who want to be there! I am a true believer that what is *for* you will *not* pass you. Keep this in mind because it can keep you in action and prevent you from freezing out of fear.

A funny thing happened to me on the way to being a multi-millionaire. When I was just starting out and coming up in the ranks, my "big whoop!" speech would ease the anxiety of my team. But once I was at the top, the response I often got was, "Well, that's easy for you to say, *Shari Brown*. You don't have to worry about your income." (They always say it as if it's one word: ShariBrown. Lol. #idigress) That one stopped me in my tracks! So let me be absolutely crystal clear: I do not have a "big whoop" attitude because of where I'm at in my career. I'm where I am in my career *because* of my "big whoop" attitude. I wouldn't have been able to survive without it. So don't think that this perspective is something that you only use when things are going your way. It's the opposite. This is the attitude to adopt when you're facing the big stuff and you're frozen in fear and overwhelm. "Big whoop" your way out of it!

Bob and Weave

In chapter 5, we talked about pivoting to prosper and how your mindset around problem solving is everything. Now it's time to bob and weave, and I'm not talking hairstyles! In boxing, to bob and weave means to make rapid movements—up and down and from side to side, for example—as an evasive tactic. Be limber, be nimble, always looking for the way out of a challenging situation.

If you expect that you are always going to face hurdles in your business, you're going to be more prepared mentally than most. If you know that you win or you learn, you're even further ahead! Hurdles aren't stop signs! At the end of the race, the person who has jumped the most hurdles has the strongest legs, right? I always look at a challenging situation as my continuing education. This doesn't mean I like challenges. Who wouldn't love a life that is always easy breezy?! But that's never going to happen, so let that dream go. #dreamkiller

We all know people (and hey, at some point many of us *were* those people) who hit a snag in their life or business and completely fall apart. Overwhelm and fear take over, and they freeze, literally and figuratively. I realized years ago that the more I sat in a bad situation, the worse it got.

I've coached so many people who want to talk endlessly about the problem, beat it to a bloody pulp, and then make a smoothie out of it. They hang on to the problem and the story like it's their new best friend. Sure, they will *tell* you that they hate the situation, they hate drama, but then they refuse to let go of it. Some people do this because they want an excuse to quit, and others do it because they are scared and don't know how to proceed. Here's what I know for sure—the problem and the solution do not occupy the same space. They don't have the same address! If you're focused on the problem, it's harder for the solution to occur to you. Think about being lost in the jungle. You're in the middle of the trees and bushes, and you can't see how to get out of it. If you're up in a helicopter, you can look down and see which direction to go to get out of that situation. You have to change your *mental* location!

I get it! Sometimes we are dealing with huge problems, and it's okay to be upset about them. But just remember that the more time you take to sit in it, the more stuck you'll feel. It's like quicksand; the longer you sit, the worse it is, and the harder it will be to get out. Visualize yourself skipping across the surface of it. You are aware that it's there, but you're focused on getting to the other side. For me, the bigger the obstacle, the faster I move. I do not want to be in a bad situation for one second longer than necessary, and so I "big whoop" my way out of it and look for the solution, or at least for some wiggle room where I can pivot and keep moving. I realize it's just another hurdle that I will get past, and it will be an entertaining Rocking Chair Story. With practice, you can get to the point where the minute a challenging situation presents itself, you instantly bob and weave to begin finding solutions.

Listen closely! Who you surround yourself with is everything! As motivational speaker and icon Jim Rohn famously noted, you are the average of the five people you spend the most time with. Think about that. (Some of you just got scared and are gonna need a moment! Lol.) If you're working hard to master a new mindset that is ready to bob and weave, focusing on the solution and not the problem, you need to surround yourself with like-minded individuals. If you don't, it's very difficult to change and grow. It's the old "crabs in a bucket" story we talked about earlier, where the crabs can't escape from a bucket because the other crabs pull them down. When you begin to grow and evolve, the people around you who want you to stay the same will make it hard for you to change. They don't always do it intentionally, but the "new you" might scare them and make them feel insecure. If you realize you're surrounded by "crabs," don't fret. You can still love them where they're at, but be mindful of how much time you're spending with them! Always be in search of others who are doing what you want to be doing and going where you want to be going in your business and in your life.

Self-care Isn't Selfish!

Theresa had been a leader for a few years. She cared so much about her team and worked hard to always be there for anything that they needed. Sounds great, right? Well, Theresa came to me for help because she was running on empty and felt like she had nothing left to give. First of all, Theresa was a chronic overreactor. The sky was always falling, and every issue, no matter how small, was a catastrophe in her mind. #lookoutchickenlittle Fear was driving the bus. As a result, she was constantly in crisis mode. Friends, we are not meant to live this way! I also realized that Theresa didn't have any boundaries, so she felt like she had to take on every issue and concern from her team—at all hours of the day and night. She was most definitely caught up in the drama. It's no wonder she was

Overwhelm
is **lack**
of a plan.

exhausted—anyone would be! But leadership doesn't have to feel that way! #deepbreath

Here are five problem-solving tips that helped Theresa get back on her feet and live life on her own terms. I think they can help you too:

1   Remember that you are selling a product, and it's not life or death. Back orders and delays will happen, and everyone will survive.

2   It's okay (and necessary) to have office hours, and they don't have to be from nine to five. They could be from 8 a.m. until 2 p.m., and then maybe you're in and out between 2 p.m. and 7 p.m. for kid pickup, homework, sports, and dinner. You are your own boss, so create what works for *you*! Plan a time for a hard stop at night, at least an hour before bed.

3   Not everything is a crisis. "Big whoop!" Remember? If you rank every issue as a 10 on a scale of 1 to 10, you'll burn out sooner rather than later. There are very few 10s, actually. If something isn't going to matter in a year, six months, or even a week from now, then it ranks below a 5. The more experience you get, the more you'll realize that *this too shall pass*. Do what is within your control, and let the rest go! I know it's hard to let go, but do it anyway. #trustme

4   Your company has a support department for a reason; let them handle as many issues as you can so you are freed up to do what only *you* can do.

5   You're here to help people build a business. And yes, it's great to become friends, but don't become everyone's therapist. Help with business issues—but let their friends and their mamas handle the other personal issues. As your team grows, it becomes increasingly difficult and taxing to be the

emotional support for everyone. Being a positive, uplifting source in their life *and* helping them build a business is plenty!

You can't pour from an empty cup, so it's important that you have strong boundaries and take care of yourself. I know it might feel selfish, but it's not. So much is depending on you, and if you fall apart, so does everything else. Your business and family need you! Recognize when you need rest, and take that time to regroup and refresh. That's why this business is so fantastic— you get to decide when you need a break! I've witnessed too many women who ended up quitting because they refused to take breaks. Not long after quitting, and once they'd had time to rest, I'd get the tearful phone calls of regret for giving up what they had worked so hard to build. And it was all because a sister just needed a break! If you listen to your body and your intuition, and take the breaks when you need them, your growth potential is limitless. She who does not quit, wins! #ferreal

The Butterfly List

Are you ready for one of the craziest, most amazing stories ever? This story is so nuts and pivotal in my life that it's not even a question of whether to share it with you. But it 100% happened, and it feels like a miracle, so I have to share it!

I was getting a massage from a lady whom I had seen a few times before. Her name was Casey, and she didn't know much about me except that I had also been a massage therapist in my former life. After the massage, Casey told me that she was very intuitive and asked me if I was open to hearing something. *Sure!* I'm always open to that sort of stuff. She told me that she had this mental picture while working on me, and she didn't know what it meant. She was wondering if it would make sense to me.

She said, "I saw a lioness who was chasing butterflies. It's a lot of energy to chase butterflies, and there's not much sustenance once you catch one, so I was scratching my head, wondering why the lioness was wasting her time and energy on all these butterflies instead of just focusing her energy on catching a meaty gazelle. Do you know what this means?" (Where are the dang emojis and gifs when I need them?!)

Oh, snap! Umm . . . *yes*. I seriously needed a moment because that image hit me like a ton of bricks and resonated with my *soul*! I was the lioness. All of the busywork in my life was the butterflies. This book was the gazelle! Up until that point, I had been trying to fit my writing into the nooks and crannies of my daily life instead of focusing on the book. As a result, I was feeling like I didn't have enough time to write, and my focus was scattered, much like chasing butterflies. That's not to say the other things in my life weren't important—they very much were—but I had been doing those things for years, so they really were on autopilot. And writing a book, while it's a huge and daunting project, is a *season* of my life. I'm not going to be writing forever, even though some days it feels like it! #Lordgivemestrength Also, books live on for a long time, and it mattered to me to pour my best into it. Energy flows where your focus goes, so it's no wonder writing had been stressful up to that point.

That image that Casey shared unlocked so much inside of me. In those few minutes that she was sharing the visual, it crystalized in my mind—what I had been doing, what I needed to change, and how I could help other women who struggle with the same thing. This is where the Butterfly List was born.

We all have our butterflies, things that use up a lot of our energy but don't give us a lot of sustenance. If you can identify what those butterflies are for you and eliminate them, you will

have more energy to focus on *your* gazelle. Now, remember—
your gazelle will change. You don't chase a gazelle forever, just
until you catch it. (I'd rather not dwell on what happens to the
gazelle next, thankyouverymuch.) Then you rest and start looking for your next one. Everything has its season, and while this
season was my book, that will come to an end (right?!), and I'll
have another season where I'll focus on another aspect of my
business.

Butterflies could be:

- Worrying about what other people think.

- Scrolling through social media.

- Unnecessarily being the support agent for your team.

- Focusing too much on your team and not enough on your
  own personal business.

- Doing things for your kids that they can do for themselves.

- Doing busywork like cleaning out your closet, or responding
  to notifications and messages on Facebook that aren't necessary (okay, that last one is me!) to avoid the next steps you
  know you should take.

- Watching too much TV when you could be going for a walk
  and listening to a book (also me!).

Gazelles could be:

- A promotion.

- A financial goal.

- A big project.

- Any goal that is meaningful.

What is your butterfly and **what is your gazelle?**

Those are just a few ideas, and I'm sure if you sat down and thought about it for five minutes, you could come up with a much longer list for yourself. If you just eliminated a few of the butterflies, can you see how much time you'd free up for yourself? I found it really helpful to keep a Butterfly List so that I could catch myself doing the things I really didn't need to be doing. I'd keep it on my desk so I could see it daily. Sometimes I had to say out loud, "Stop it, Shari!" There's something about saying things out loud that really gives them more impact, don't ya think?!

You can achieve anything that you *decide* you want to achieve! Everything you do should be leading you in the direction of that gazelle. Remember, it's a season; it's not forever. Sometimes your gazelle might be a business goal, but sometimes it's going to be mental, physical, or emotional wellness, and sometimes it's going to be related to your family. Whatever it is, it gets most of your focus and energy for that season. That doesn't mean you ignore the other areas of your life! But, for example, when my book is my gazelle, it gets my extra oomph! It is my goal, and so it's the first thing I work on every day, and when I get my hour of writing done, I move on to the other areas. (I'll let you in on a little secret: I've told myself that fitness will be my gazelle when this book is finished. That one will be just as challenging as writing for me. #ugh #whydoIhateitsomuch)

As women, we juggle so many things at once, every day! We don't have the luxury of balance. I think balance is bullshit, quite frankly. #pardonmyFrench Instead we have priorities, and they shuffle often, sometimes hourly! You could have a business goal and a very important day planned, but then a kid gets sick, and—boom!—everything changes. It's what makes women badasses in business because multitasking is in our DNA. But if we don't identify what our goal is (gazelle) and what's wasting our time and energy (butterflies), then we could get to the end of our day, week, month, or even year, wonder why we are so damn tired, and realize we have nothing to show for that exhaustion!

Goals and Habits

I mentioned that my initial goal in my business was to earn enough money to get one mani/pedi per month. I'm a big believer in aiming low! Small goals for quick wins can lead to big achievements and a joyful journey. So I'm not going to harp on big fat audacious goals. (Some people call them big hairy audacious goals, but I don't understand why they have to be hairy.) #ewwwgross I think dreaming big is a lot of fun, but only if that dream brings you joy! If it causes your butt to twitch, then back off because you'll end up freezing... or maybe that's just me! #letthebutttwitchbeyourguide. If you can think of your goal, break it down into small steps, and *then* come up with the daily habits that will help you achieve those steps, you will absolutely hit that goal! It's impossible not to.

So, spend some time mapping out your goals and habits. I recommend a simple system that starts by identifying your yearly goal, and then breaking that down into monthly and then weekly goals. The process looks like this:

1 Write down your yearly goal.

2 Write down monthly goals that will get you to your yearly goal.

3 Each month, break down the weekly goals that will achieve your monthly goal.

I stop at weekly goals because it's too easy to get discouraged when you have a daily goal and then life happens, and you find yourself going a day or two without achieving those goals and feel like you're behind. It's too easy to get discouraged and then give up before you've even finished your first week. I'm all about small wins to set you up for success!

Let's say that your business goal is to build your customer base. Using the simple steps above, mapping out your goals could look like this:

1 Yearly goal: gain 100 new clients.

2 Monthly goal: add about eight new clients each month.

3 Weekly goal: add two new customers a week.

This is where habits now come into play. What daily habits can you develop to achieve that weekly goal, which will lead to the monthly goal and eventually the yearly goal? Here are some ideas:

- Comment on the posts and stories of 20-plus people each day, using four or more words and asking questions to encourage engagement when possible. (This improves your algorithm!)

- Join Facebook groups that discuss hobbies and topics you're interested in.

- Comment on five or more of the posts from the people in these groups. (Remember, do not ever mention your business in the group! You are there to make friends. When you later post about your business on your own profile, they will see the post.)

- Post and/or go live on social media to show products.

- Follow up with past customers. Don't forget to ask for referrals!

The power of these daily habits is in the consistency. The more consistent you are, the more effective they are! What might take you an hour to do in the beginning will take less time the more you do it because you'll get really good at it. Connecting with new people will become second nature. Every giant goal is achievable when it's broken down into the smallest of habits and then repeated often. If you want to grow quicker in your business, do more activity. Remember, lots of activity in a short period of time creates momentum! #vroomvroom

Grow for It!

It's Okay to Be Rich

Growing up, what were you taught about money and rich people? Most of us know exactly how our families feel about "the wealthy." We heard the comments in our homes, from our parents and other family members. Maybe you were raised hearing that wealthy people were faceless CEOs in suits, with yachts, who only cared about themselves. Cold and heartless. This is a common view of wealthy people if you don't grow up knowing any. Our mindsets around money can run deep. It is so important that we get our judgments around money in alignment with our goals, because otherwise we could be sabotaging our business without even realizing it.

Family stories around money matter because a funny thing can happen when you start earning money. Whatever messages you were given about wealth can creep back up. You may not even be aware of your money mindset, so it's important to investigate because it can hold you back. If you were brought up believing that people with money were bad people, you will be more likely to sabotage your own success. Because who wants to be a cold, heartless person? Nobody I know!

I don't know about you, but I wasn't raised with money. We were very middle class, and at times even that was a stretch. My dad had a blue-collar job, and my mom stayed home with us. I never thought we were poor, but I knew money was tight. Looking back, I can see how my mom tried to stretch a dollar, using half a pound of hamburger for tacos and the other half for spaghetti sauce the next night. That's not a lot of meat for a family of four! I also remember someone teasing me at school when I was in the fourth grade, because I wore the same shoes to school every day. Ummm... what?! Those were my school shoes, and the only shoes I had. Thankfully, that *joke* went right over my head at nine years old. Even though we didn't have a lot of money, my parents were generous people. They gave at church and to people less fortunate, when they could, and that made a big impact on me.

I remember how amazing it felt to know that we had helped another family in some way. Many of those moments are crystal clear in my memory, and I'm very grateful for them because they shaped my focus as I began to make money. Generosity became a big part of my motivation to grow a business and earn as much money as I was capable of earning. The more I earn, the more I can give.

Now, I'm not suggesting that you give away the farm. No way! I've seen lots of that, and that is a self-worth issue, when you feel like you don't deserve the money that you've earned. Take care of yourself and your family *first*, and then figure out a percentage that you want to give to your favorite charities. As you receive, give a percentage, but don't give to your own detriment.

I've had jobs where I wasn't paid what I was worth, and that sucked. And then I had a job where I was paid way more than I ever dreamed I was worth. That doesn't suck, but it can mess with your head! Joe Vitale, a Law of Attraction expert and spiritual teacher, said, "Money will always match your mindset," so when I found myself making really good money, I was determined that I wouldn't let any preconceived notions about wealth sabotage my success. I want the best money mindset I can have, don't you? Of all the obstacles to making money, *I* sure don't want to be a part of the problem!

Here's how I know that these money mindset issues run deep. It was several years into my business, and I was already a multimillion-dollar earner. One day in December I had taken my daughter to school and decided to run by Target to grab some wrapping paper for Christmas. I had a really busy day ahead of me, and as I pulled into the parking lot, I realized that I had forgotten to see how much wrapping paper I already had to know how much I needed to buy. Now I had to go home to look and then come all the way back to Target. *Ugh!*

As I was pulling out of the Target parking lot, I slapped myself. (Well, not literally!) Hellooo, Shari Brown! You do *not* have to go home to count wrapping paper rolls. You can afford to *treat yoself* and buy as many rolls of wrapping paper as your heart desires! Seriously, they were $3 each! (I actually went live and did a training for my team on this very day! Check it out: youtube.com/watch?v=Q3OzXsufG8k.)

It may sound funny, but in my mind, wrapping paper was expensive and it shouldn't be wasted. I still don't like to waste things, no matter how much money I make, but sometimes when you're in a time crunch, money can buy you the freedom to have options. I was stunned at how deep that mindset was in me. I was oblivious to it until it smacked me in my face! #oldhabitsdiehard

I want you to know that it is okay to be rich. I want you to know that not only is it okay, but it's a really, really good thing, *especially* if you grew up thinking that rich people were bad and selfish. Because you aren't bad and selfish, right?! So wouldn't it be *amazing* if someone who has a kind and giving heart was rich? Nothing in this world feels better than being able to give. The more you make, the more you can help!

Here's my hope for you—I want you to go out into the world and work to your full potential with all your heart, and then I want you to accept the fruits of your labor with joy and gratitude for the opportunities you've had. Once you've done that and your financial situation is rock solid, turn around and help someone else do it. That is the best duplication in the world!

If you are one of the lucky ones who has never struggled with money mindset issues, *fantastic*!! Just keep these stories I've shared in mind as you grow your team because I guarantee you will run across many people who do struggle with this, and now you will be able to help them!

The Game Plan

As you charge ahead in your business, I want you to be realistic with your expectations. Don't expect maximum results for minimal input. This isn't a get-rich-quick scheme; it's a business. And in my opinion, having worked in various other business models, it's the best one because of the flexibility and opportunities it affords. It's so much better than a retail model because you don't have to pay overhead for a building, and you're not bogged down with tons of expenses. You're self-employed, so you get to choose how to run your business. Here are three basic options. Picture it like this: There are three lanes on the Business Building Superhighway.

- The Slow Lane: This lane is for the dabbler and the hobbyist who enjoys the discount and maybe occasionally sells something to a friend or family member. She might exit and enter the Business Building Superhighway frequently.

A goal without a plan is just a wish. Be clear on how to proceed.

- The Middle Lane: This lane is for the person who works her business part-time, ten to 20 hours per week. She is pretty consistent and interested in earning money to supplement her household income. She is making the car payment, or paying for utilities, groceries, kids' sports, school clothes, and family outings.

- The Fast Lane: This lane is for the woman who is not messing around. She works this gig full-time, and she wants a full-time income. She's working 40-plus hours a week, and she's all in! Her income is paying the mortgage, paying for college, the 401k, all of the big stuff.

No matter what lane you're in, there's room at the table for you! That's the beauty of network marketing. It fits in wherever you want it to fit in. From baseball games to beaches, whether you live in the city or the country—if you have Internet and a phone, you can build a business!

Here are four hot tips for making the most of the time you *do* have and being the most productive *you* possible:

1   Turn off all notifications on your phone. When you're working, you're checking email and messages regularly anyway, so you don't need a pop-up notification. Notifications are like being pecked to death by a chicken! It will burn you out in the long run!

2   Set productive office hours. Timers are your friend! You will tend to stay more focused on the task at hand when you know there is a time limit. So set your timer and get to work!

3   Slow your scroll. Stay off your newsfeed during work hours! It is the world's biggest time suck. Instead, work with intention by going to your list of friends and finding the people you haven't seen in a while. Then go to their profile wall to comment or send a message.

4 Use a planner. People don't plan to fail; they fail to plan! And remember that overwhelm is simply lack of a plan. So write down what you want to accomplish this week, or this month, and then work backwards by mapping out those tasks and daily habits that will help you get to your weekly and monthly goals!

Find the Joy in *Your* Journey

No matter what your goals are, make them personal to *you*! Don't worry about the promotion if that's not what drives you. You can blaze any trail that you like; there are no rules. Make your "why" bigger than yourself, and since you have the power to run your business any way that you want, *choose* to find some joy every day and incorporate it into your business. The joy isn't found just at the top of the company or in the next promotion. There is joy to be found every day if you decide to find it—or create it!

As a recovering jack-of-all-trades, I can tell you what this business is not. It is not Disneyland. It is not a get-rich-quick scheme or a pyramid scheme or any of that nonsense. It is a business model, just like retail and wholesale. This one happens to be direct to consumer. Because of that, there's a lot of potential to earn the money that would typically be spent in advertising and paying the middlemen. But ultimately it is a job, and like all jobs, there are highs and lows, things you love and things you don't. If you expect that, you'll be better able to manage it all. Revel in the highs—but know they won't last. Pivot during the lows—knowing that they won't last either!

What I love the most about the network marketing business is that it can be whatever you want it to be for *you*. The creative possibilities are endless! You can blaze a trail and try things that have never been done before, and even if you fall short, you've learned and garnered some killer street cred from your fellow entrepreneurs. #highfive And if you succeed... you've garnered some mad street cred from your fellow entrepreneurs. #nothinbutnet Nobody is judging you as harshly as you've been judging yourself; I promise. #respectthehustle

Go be *you* and shine your light because you're an inspiration even if you don't know it yet! Your future is bright, and one consistent baby step at a time is all it's going to take. I believe in you!

You *grow*, girl! xo

Acknowledgments

FIRST OF all, I'd like to thank my husband and my kids for their patience with me as I took on yet another big project, and they had to deal with mama being very busy and often stressed. I love you all so much! Thanks for letting me spread my wings. To Derek Maxfield, without your vision and heart, I wouldn't have been able to fulfill my own dreams! Blessed to be on this journey with you, my friend! To my *amazing* team of Younique Presenters, I wouldn't be here without you. Thank you for your trust in me over the years, and thank you for your heart and your hustle! I could only lead if you were willing to follow. To the *most* amazing, loyal followers on the planet, *thank you* for your kindness and friendship, for showing up to #FridayFBLive every week, and for supporting this book! It is my absolute pleasure to serve you!

To Gabby Bernstein, thank you! You don't even know how God used you to nudge me in this direction, and without that nudge I would never have met Richelle Fredson. Oh, Richelle! I cannot say enough about you, your wisdom, your straight talk, and your guidance. This book would not be what it is without you. Working with you was like taking a MasterClass in all things writing and publishing! You are the backbone of this book, and I am forever grateful that I found you. #friendsforever To Tori Poulter, thanks for your counsel and friendship, for giving me clarity and focus throughout this journey, and for having the idea for the Butterfly List! What a gift you have been to me. To the Page Two team—Jesse, Adrineh, Kendra, and the incredible designers, distributors, and marketers—wow! Just *wow*. Your care and support have been next level! Thanks for holding my hand every step of the way and caring about this book as much as I do. I know that this is the first of many projects together, and I can't wait to see what the future holds. Just let me nap for a sec first, k? ;)

About the Author

SHARI IS a stay-at-home mom turned multimillionaire! With a background in retail sales and management, Shari joined Younique, a network marketing company, in 2013. Her only intention was to sell enough makeup to afford a mani/pedi once a month. A little over a year later, Shari became Younique's first Mascara Millionaire! After over eight years with the company, she has continued to be one of the top earners, with a team of over 400,000 women who have collectively sold over $600 million in products to date. Affectionately referred to as "Mama Shari" for her tough-lovin', straight-talkin' approach to training, she has garnered more than 15 million views of her Facebook Lives just in the last few years! Her leadership and relatability have led her to speaking engagements for tens of thousands of women all over the United States, Canada, and Europe. Shari lives in a small town in Southern California with her husband, two children, and Bella the dog.

Let's continue the conversation! Here's how to find me:

Website: sharibrown.com. Sign up to stay connected and receive my newsletter, book tour dates, and more!

Facebook: facebook.com/shariowenbrown. Follow me! #Friday-FBLive trainings happen every... well, Friday! #duh

Instagram: @shariowenbrown. Honestly, I'm really bad at IG, but it's on my to-do list. Better follow me on Facebook first! #keepinitreal

YouTube: youtube.com/c/ShariBrown678. This is a great resource to find my content and get a good laugh at my old stuff!

Audible version of _Let's Grow, Girl!_ That's right, you can have me preaching right to ya because this book is available as an audiobook on Audible and other platforms!

Bulk orders: Want to give _Let's Grow, Girl!_ to your team? Contact us at sharibrown.com/book to arrange a bulk order!

If you enjoyed this book and its message, please consider offering your review on Amazon, Goodreads, or your favorite online forum. #muchobliged

CPSIA information can be obtained
at www.ICGtesting.com
Printed in the USA
LVHW110138180622
721553LV00003B/5